*From Garden to Table*

# GROWING & COOKING
# WITH HERBS

## From Garden to Table

# GROWING & COOKING
# WITH HERBS

*Pamela Thomas*

*A Random House/Friedman Group Book*

**A FRIEDMAN GROUP BOOK**

This 1991 edition published by
Random House of Canada Limited
1265 Aerowood Drive
Mississauga, Ontario L4W 1B9
Canada

Canadian Cataloging-in-Publication Data
Thomas, Pamela, 1946–
Growing & cooking with herbs

(From garden to table series)
ISBN 0-394-22152-4

1. Herb gardening.   2. Cookery (Herbs).   I. Title
II. Series: Thomas, Pamela, 1946–  . From garden to table series.

SB351.T48 1991   641.3′57   C90-095247-4

*FROM GARDEN TO TABLE*
*GROWING AND COOKING WITH HERBS*
was prepared and produced by
Michael Friedman Publishing Group, Inc.
15 West 26th Street
New York, New York 10010

Editor: Melissa Schwarz
Art Director: Jeff Batzli
Designer: Lynne Yeamans
Photo Researcher: Daniella Jo Nilva

Typeset by The Interface Group, Inc.
Color separation by Excel Graphic Arts Co.
Printed and bound in Hong Kong by LeeFung-Asco Printers Limited

8 7 6 5 4 3 2 1

© Derek Fell

© Derek Fell

# CONTENTS

# ACKNOWLEDGMENTS

*Although I worked on many gardening books during my years as an editor, I had never written one. This was my first—and a special treat for me because herbs hold a very special place in my heart and in my palate.*

*I would like to thank several people at the Michael Friedman Group for giving me the opportunity to write this book and for helping to create such a lovely "product." Melissa Schwarz, my editor, provided immense patience and intelligence as I shaped and wrote the manuscript. Liz Sullivan, Sharyn Rosart, and Karla Olson provided additional editorial support and guidance. Lynne Yeamans pulled it all together with an attractive design and a fine selection of art and photography.*

*Several people shared their recipes with me, including Susan Costner, John Hadamuscin, Anne Seranne, Rozanne Gold, Waldy Malouf, Mary Gubser, and Ronald Johnson. Their work enhances this book immeasurably and I thank them for their generosity.*

*Finally, I'd like to thank Patty, Rick, and Abbie Layne for permitting me to invade their backyard.*

# INTRODUCTION

*Gardening with herbs is one of the most pleasurable aspects of working with plants and the earth. Not only are herbs beautiful to look at, they are relatively easy to grow and serve a multitude of purposes—from settling an upset stomach to providing a fresh, flowery fragrance in the garden and the house to elevating a simple supper to a magnificent feast.*

*Since ancient times, scholars have studied the various aspects of herbs, and few have neglected to note that herbs provide perhaps the most marvelous grace note to cooking. And that is what this book is about: The pleasures of growing herbs, and then using them creatively, naturally, and delectably in the kitchen.*

9

*This symmetrical herb garden is enhanced by the addition of a wooden bench.*

© Anita Sabarese

Herbs have been a topic of conversation and cultivation since the beginning of time. In the *Book of Genesis,* plants served as symbols of life, and the humble herb has held its own as both a symbol and a fact in the physical, mental, and spiritual development of mankind.

Virtually every culture throughout the world has developed a special interest in herbs. "Herbals"—books about the properties of various herbs—have existed in one form or another for five thousand years.

Babylonian tablets from 3000 B.C. illustrated medical treatments using herbs. Over the next millennia, Chinese, Egyptian, Indian, and Assyrian cultures recorded developments using herbs for medicinal purposes.

Many cultures—and most herbals—stressed the practical aspects of herbs, not only their medicinal properties but their other uses. Herbs could be used to freshen the home, dye fabrics, create perfumes or skin lotions, or decorate a room, a church, or the human form. Many philosophers and priests noted the "mystical" qualities of certain herbs, and thus many herbs were also used for religious purposes such as church decoration (sweet woodruff) or as sacred symbols (meadowsweet).

Herbs are mentioned in relation to cooking as early as the first century B.C. by the Roman epicure, Apicius. Herbs remained a staple in European cooking for the next fifteen hundred years, but like art, music, and literature, enjoyed a "renaissance" in Europe in the sixteenth and seventeenth centuries. At that time, gardening, in general, was studied seriously as an art (and as a science), and herbs emerged as central to that study.

Interest in gardening and cooking ebbs and flows, but in recent years, especially in the United States and Canada, fascination with both fields has soared. North Americans have developed more sophisticated palates and a greater concern for health, natural foods, ecology, and the environment. Herbs relate to and address all these issues.

Herbs provide a fascinating combination of beauty and practicality. For the most part, herbs are easy to grow and harvest. They are a perfect introduction to gardening, yet can challenge the expert.

Herb gardens can be as simple as a miniscule window garden containing half a dozen plants. They can also be as complex as the large and glamorous beds designed in the classic, seventeenth-century manner still seen at grand houses such as Mount Vernon or Monticello.

Herb gardens can be built around themes, with the plants symbolizing the subject at hand. One can create a Shakespearean herb garden, growing only those plants mentioned in the Bard's plays, such as columbine, calendula, myrtle, or wormwood. One can indulge in a heady sense of smell and cultivate a garden of fragrances, focusing on marjoram, hyssop, jasmine, sweet woodruff, and bayberry. One could be practical and grow herbs for such utilitarian purposes as making natural dyes (indigo, saffron, violet, and bloodroot) or manufacturing teas (angelica, lemon verbena, chamomile, or thyme). Or, as we are doing here, one can focus on the culinary herbs (oregano, dill, bay, basil, rosemary—and many more) that turn one of the necessities of everyday life into a sybaritic indulgence.

For the cook, herbs offer endless opportunities for creativity in the kitchen. Many classic recipes (such as béarnaise sauce) depend upon the flavor of a particular herb (in this case, tarragon). But a meticulous choice of herb can transform the simplest egg dish, the most mundane roast chicken, or humblest dessert into a unique and masterful delight. Thus, this book helps to create a double pleasure—the joy of growing herbs and the bliss of eating—in both ordinary and extraordinary ways.

— *Part I* —

# HERBS IN THE GARDEN

# Chapter 1

## PLANNING AND CULTIVATING A CULINARY HERB GARDEN

*Opposite: A stone walk through an informal herb garden. Right: Lush plantings of sage, artemisia, and rosemary around a stone sundial.*

© Joanne Pavia

*Herbs are like good children. They are cooperative plants—easy to sow, reasonably simple to cultivate, and happy if they are planned for properly and cared for once they arrive. They have relatively simple wants and needs, and learning about those needs is easy for the gardener.*

15

© Joanne Pavia

*A large and casual country herb garden containing artemisia, lavender, and other country herbs.*

## CHOOSING A SITE

The first step toward planning an herb garden is evaluating the site where your garden and your herbs will grow. You must consider your climate (especially the prevailing temperature) and select the herbs that grow best in that climate. You must also analyze the landscape or topography of your property, the surrounding architec-

ture, the sunlight, the availability of water, and the condition of the soil.

Climate is initially the most important factor to consider when planning an herb garden—or any garden for that matter. The U.S. Department of Agriculture has divided North America into ten zones based on the average minimum winter temperatures of the respective zone, Zone 1 being the coldest and Zone 10 the warmest (see map, page 17). Before planning a garden, one must know one's zone and select herbs that will thrive in that climate.

Herbs are categorized as annual, biennial, and perennial. Annuals, or plants that last for one season, are characterized as tender, half-hardy, or hardy. These descriptions reflect the plant's relationship to the prevailing climate. Tender annuals will not tolerate frost or cold weather; half-hardy plants will grow in cooler weather; hardy annuals will survive heavy frost. Biennials (plants that take two growing seasons to complete their life cycle) and perennials (plants that die down in winter and re-bloom in spring) are also evaluated in relation to their ability to survive in particular climatic zones. Since perennials remain in the earth year after year, their hardiness must be considered particularly carefully.

The climate or temperature of the garden is also affected by individual topography and architecture. A garden located on a windy slope may be cooler than a garden found in the same zone that sits in a shel-

# USDA Plant Hardiness Zone Map

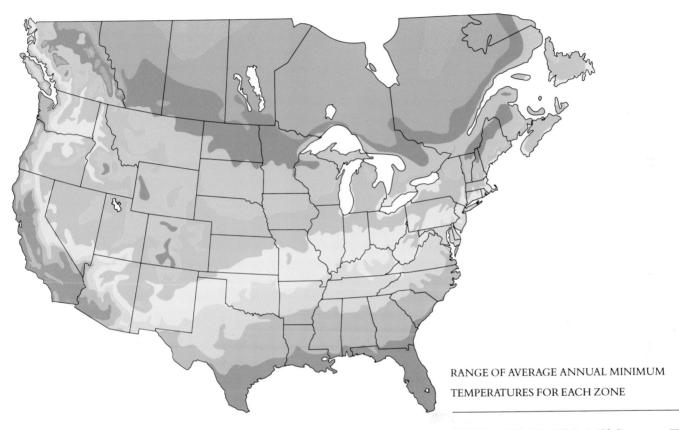

RANGE OF AVERAGE ANNUAL MINIMUM
TEMPERATURES FOR EACH ZONE

| ZONE 1 | BELOW –50° F | (–45° C) | |
| ZONE 2 | –50° TO –40° | (–45° to –40°) | |
| ZONE 3 | –40° TO –30° | (–40° to –34°) | |
| ZONE 4 | –30° TO –20° | (–34° to –28°) | |
| ZONE 5 | –20° TO –10° | (–28° to –23°) | |
| ZONE 6 | –10° TO   0° | (–23° to –17°) | |
| ZONE 7 |   0° TO  10° | (–17° to –12°) | |
| ZONE 8 |  10° TO  20° | (–12° to –6°) | |
| ZONE 9 |  20° TO  30° | (–6° to –1°) | |
| ZONE 10 |  30° TO  40° | (–1° to 4°) | |

© Robert Perron

*An herb garden designed in a formal style.*

tered valley. A garden enclosed by a wall, fence, or building may be able to support plants that would not otherwise grow well in that zone. On the other hand, a fence or building may block sun, depriving the plants of both light and warmth. These issues are sometimes referred to as micro-climates, and must also be considered when planning the garden scheme.

Sunlight is of primary importance to most herbs. With some exceptions like sweet woodruff, which flourishes in shade, herbs require a minimum of six to eight hours of sunlight each day, although these requirements vary from plant to plant. Check individual plant descriptions in *Part II, A Culinary Herbal,* for sunlight require-ments, then select your plants according to the availability of sunlight on your site.

Herbs require certain water and soil con-ditions, but for the most part, these are not difficult to supply or monitor. Again, check the particular plant descriptions for the details on watering and soil preparation.

Finally, consider your personal concerns with regard to your garden. Do you want your garden to serve as a restful retreat? Do you wish your herbs to be growing within easy reach of a busy kitchen? Do you want a bountiful crop with plenty of herbs left over to dry and freeze? Do you want a for-mal or casual style? Or do you want a more modest garden that is easier to maintain? When planning the site and size of your garden, bear these questions in mind.

# DESIGNING THE GARDEN

Once you have selected your garden site, you must then design it carefully. Designing the garden can be a pleasurable—and challenging—task. Again, there are many considerations. Do you want a formal garden, based on classic geometric patterns and shapes like the diamond, the Elizabethan knot, the cartwheel, or the square-within-a-square? Do you want an informal garden with herbs casually falling over into flower beds or interspersed with vegetables? Do you want to incorporate herbs into a hedge or edging? Or do you want to combine styles for a modern, eclectic effect?

You must also think carefully about the types of plants you wish to cultivate. Are they tall and willowy or low to the ground and bushy? Do they flower? What about color? Do you want all perennials? Or all annuals? Do you want a purely culinary garden, or do you want to add some additional herbs for other purposes?

Herb gardens can be designed and grown in a multitude of ways. They can be mixed in with flowers or vegetables; planted as borders, edging, or ground covers; or grown in pots or containers on terraces or decks. They can be carefully pruned and controlled to create a classic shape or permitted to flourish in a more easygoing style. Or, they can be grown in a mixture of styles.

*Above: When designing a garden, consider adding a path, a seat, or an element like this beehive to establish a focal point. Left: A formal herb garden designed in the square-within-a-square pattern. The brick walkway and the handsome sundial make this a particularly attractive garden.*

*A classic herb garden designed in a cartwheel pattern.*

*A formal herb garden combining the square-within-a-square pattern with the love knot design.*

Before you buy any plants or seeds, thoroughly research your garden conditions, including sunlight, soil, drainage, and architectural conditions or needs. Also, think about the amount of space you have, the amount of time you wish to devote to maintenance, the extent of your desired crop, and the overall appearance of the garden itself.

### Drawing a Garden Plan

For best results, it is imperative that you draw a detailed garden plan. Using a grid, measure the outlines of the overall site and mark immovable fixtures such as fences, patios, large trees, or buildings. Also note changes in level that might affect plant growth and therefore require terracing, steps, or raised beds.

Using tracing paper, experiment with different plans, taking into consideration the style you wish your garden to take, the number and kind of plants you want to grow, and the garden's relationship to the rest of the site and the surrounding house or other architectural features. Don't forget to include paths and walkways so that the herbs are easily accessible as you plant the garden or harvest your crop. Remember, too, that the paths can reflect the style of the garden—whether they are gravel, brick, grassy, stone, or even wood—and should blend well with the overall garden style.

A focal point to the garden is often an important factor. Consider adding a garden seat, a sundial, a small pool, a large urn, or a piece of statuary.

Work out the planting scheme carefully. Appraise the requirements of the plants themselves, taking into account leaf size and color, plant shapes and heights. Try to plant perennials in places where they will not be jostled as they rest over the winter, and group the same genus of plant, such as mints, together in one place.

Once the soil has been prepared (see page 24), transfer the design to the ground, marking the boundaries of the plot with stakes and the beds and paths with string markers or lime.

### Patty and Rick's Garden

The garden on page 23 is a culinary herb garden designed by Patty and Rick Layne, who live in suburban Washington, D.C. Patty Layne is an avid and creative cook, and she wanted to plant as many herbs as possible.

Geographically, the Laynes live in Zone 7, a somewhat temperate zone whose minimum temperature is 0 to 10 degrees F (-18 to -12 degrees C). They have a relatively small yard, so in addition to a traditional rectangular herb garden, they also have planted herbs in borders and in pots on their deck to take maximum advantage of their planting space.

The focal point of their property is a large and lovely maple tree, but unfortunately (for planting considerations), the tree shades much of the yard. As a result, the Laynes located their primary herb plot at the back of the yard, where it was not convenient to the kitchen, but was situated well away from the shaded area. However, Patty took advantage of the shady tree's benefits and planted a plot of sweet woodruff and violets around its base.

The Laynes' backyard faces south, receiving strong morning sun but, because of the tree, it gets less late-afternoon light. Their property is also surrounded by a tall wooden fence that protects their garden and their deck and helps shelter their plantings.

The primary herb plot, located in the back of the yard, is made of three small rectangles, each 4 feet by 6 feet (120 cm × 180 cm) with 2-foot (60-cm) wide gravel paths in between each plot. Patty used bricks to create a border around the outer edges of the plot. She selected brick since the Laynes' house and garage are made of brick, and the brick border seemed both easy to work with and attractive in the context of their property. (Patty considered using timbers from their recently constructed deck, which would have been equally good-looking.) She also added a brick edge in front of the east border, but left the south border open, so that the lavender that is planted there could grow in a more natural way, overflowing the border.

In the primary garden, Patty planted ten herbs: sorrel, chives, tarragon, marjoram, oregano, sage, coriander, chervil, dill, and parsley. Since she and Rick enjoy salads, she added two lettuces (romaine and Boston) and arugula.

Patty also planted herbs along the borders. On the south border she planted a few sunflowers and hyssop, and a thick border of lavender. On the east edge of the yard, she planted rosemary, lovage, and two varieties of thyme.

Patty and Rick lived in Rome for several years, and while in Europe they collected many beautiful pottery containers. They found two unusual wall pots, or lavabos, that Patty attached to the wall of the brick garage and filled with basil. Under the pots, she planted daisies and nasturtiums, and a small plot of catnip. (Patty and Rick are not the only gourmands in their family; their cat, Abby, also prefers fresh herbs.)

On their large deck, Patty took another of her large Italian pots and filled it with two varieties of mint. She also bought a bay laurel tree that she keeps on the deck during the warmer months, and moves indoors when winter arrives.

Thus, with creative planning and planting, Patty and Rick have been able to cultivate over twenty herbs in a relatively small space, and could accommodate even more varieties if they wished. On the other hand, this is a very ambitious garden design, and could be reduced and simplified by cultivating only one or two of the primary planting beds.

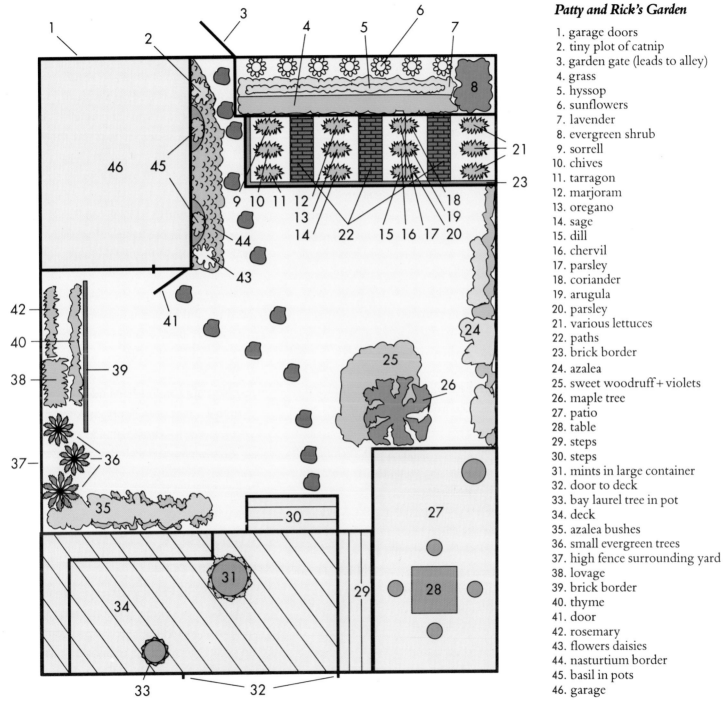

## Patty and Rick's Garden

1. garage doors
2. tiny plot of catnip
3. garden gate (leads to alley)
4. grass
5. hyssop
6. sunflowers
7. lavender
8. evergreen shrub
9. sorrell
10. chives
11. tarragon
12. marjoram
13. oregano
14. sage
15. dill
16. chervil
17. parsley
18. coriander
19. arugula
20. parsley
21. various lettuces
22. paths
23. brick border
24. azalea
25. sweet woodruff + violets
26. maple tree
27. patio
28. table
29. steps
30. steps
31. mints in large container
32. door to deck
33. bay laurel tree in pot
34. deck
35. azalea bushes
36. small evergreen trees
37. high fence surrounding yard
38. lovage
39. brick border
40. thyme
41. door
42. rosemary
43. flowers daisies
44. nasturtium border
45. basil in pots
46. garage

# PREPARING THE SOIL

Preparing the soil properly is very important for the success of your herb garden, particularly if you are growing perennials that may live in one spot for years. As with light and water, soil requirements vary from herb to herb. Some require dry soil in order to flourish, while others prefer moist conditions. Many herbs grow extremely well in what is considered poor soil—in other words, soil that is not rich in organic matter. Others may require added nutrients that are easily added by using peat moss, compost, or dehydrated manure. (Again, check the plant descriptions in *A Culinary Herbal* for particular needs.)

All herbs require well-drained soil. If soil retains puddles for several hours after rain, add organic matter, coarse grit, horticultural sand, gypsum, perlite, or vermiculite to the top 12-inch layer of soil. If the condition is problematic, consider growing your herbs in raised beds.

Most herbs—particularly the Mediterranean herbs such as oregano and marjoram—do not require large amounts of fertilizer. Nevertheless, it is wise to fertilize once or twice a year: in the spring when you are planting, and perhaps once again in midsummer. A balanced, complete mixture of fertilizer (5 percent nitrogen, 10 percent phosphate, 5 percent potash, or 5-10-5 mixture) works best.

The relative acidity or alkalinity of the soil, the pH factor, is also an important consideration. The pH of the soil is a measure of the plant's ability to absorb nutrients, and is measured on a scale of 1 to 14, 1 being the most acidic, 7 being neutral, and 14 the most alkaline. To measure the pH of soil, buy a test kit at a garden supply store or have your soil tested at a soil-testing lab.

Most herbs prefer a slightly alkaline to neutral soil with a pH level of 7 to 8. However, if you choose a plant that needs acid soil, lower the pH by adding sulfur. Also, many fertilizers are slightly acid and will lower pH somewhat. To make soil more alkaline, add lime, but only in the lowest amount. Ashes from wood fires work well to make soil more alkaline.

In early spring, test the soil's readiness for planting by using the old-fashioned farmer's method: Pick up a handful of soil and squeeze it. If it remains in a tight ball, it is still too wet; if it feels dry and dusty, it needs to be watered deeply for several days before working. If it crumbles easily, it is ready to be worked.

Till the area to be worked to a depth of about 12 inches (30 cm). (If you are planting a large plot you may want to rent a Rototiller for a day from your garden center.) Adjust the pH of the soil if necessary; add fertilizer; and if drainage is a problem, mix in perlite, vermiculite, or another material to remedy the problem. Once the soil is ready, you may sow seeds or plant.

# SOWING SEEDS

Herbs have a wide variety of planting requirements. Some can be started from seeds sown in the garden; others need to be started indoors and then replanted. Still others are very difficult to cultivate and should be purchased as plants or seedlings or propagated through cuttings.

### Starting Seeds Indoors

Plants with delicate seeds or those that require a long growing season must be started indoors. Most annual herbs (as well as certain biennials and perennials that are grown as annuals) should be started from seeds six to eight weeks before they are put outdoors in the garden.

To grow seeds indoors, use flats or small pots that are 2½ to 4 inches (6 to 10 cm) deep with good drainage holes. Flats and containers can be used from year to year, but must be rinsed thoroughly after each use. Herbs like anise that do not transplant easily should be started in peat pots, which are small pots made of pressed peat moss that can be put directly in the earth without removing the plant itself. Thus, the roots will be only mildly disturbed when they are moved outdoors.

Fill the flats or pots with a soilless medium made up of 50 percent peat moss and 50 percent perlite or vermiculite. Avoid using soil or old medium to start seeds

*Top: Starting seeds indoors in plastic trays or flats. Bottom: Various types of pots—plastic, peat, and ceramic—for starting seeds indoors.*

since they may be contaminated with disease—a sowing medium should always be sterile.

Fill the containers to within ¼ inch (.6 cm) of the top, moisten the medium, and sow the seeds according to seed packet directions. Cover the flats or pots with clear plastic or glass, and place them in a warm, well-lighted spot.

After the seeds have germinated, remove the plastic bag or glass and move the containers into full sun, or place them under fluorescent grow lights, for 12 to 14 hours per day. Water the plants from the bottom as the medium dries out, and fertilize the seedlings after they have sprouted about a half-dozen leaves. If you are using flats, transplant seedlings into individual pots at this time.

Before planting the seedlings in the garden, you will need to harden off the plants. (Hardening off means preparing the plants for their new life in the outdoors.) For one week before transplanting, move the plants to a protected spot outdoors for several hours during the day, and bring them back in at night. Each day, increase the length of time they remain outdoors. Seedlings can also be hardened off in a cold frame, which is a bottomless box set in the ground with a removable transparent top. You can buy a cold frame at your local garden center, or make one easily by constructing a box from wood and using an old storm window as a lid.

### Starting Seeds Outdoors

Some plants can be sown directly into the garden. Sow tender annuals only after all danger of frost has passed; sow half-hardy or hardy annuals in early spring depending upon your zone and whether or not they can tolerate frost. Sow biennials and perennial seeds anytime from spring through midsummer.

Some gardeners scatter seeds at random, but usually it is best to sow seeds in neat rows. It is also a good idea to label them so that you know precisely which plant is planted in a particular spot. Keep soil moist until the seeds have germinated. When plants are 2 to 3 inches (5 to 7.5 cm) high, it is time to thin them to the spacing recommended for the particular plant.

## PLANTING

Some herbs are difficult to grow from seed, and therefore you must buy them. Treat store-bought herbs as you would your own delicate seedlings. Try to plant them immediately, but if you are unable to put them in the ground right away, place them in pots or flats in partial shade and check them daily.

Plant tender annuals in mid-spring after any danger of frost has passed; plant half-hardy herbs two to four weeks before the last spring frost; and plant hardy plants one to two months before the last frost. Plant biennials and perennials that are to be grown as annuals (in other words, those which are at their best for only one season) as early in spring as possible. Biennials and perennials can be planted almost anytime, but always put them in the ground at least four weeks before the first autumn frost is due to arrive.

Plants tend to be shocked when they are first put into the ground, so try to plant in the late afternoon or on a cloudy day to ease the transplanting trauma. Remove the plants from their containers carefully, and avoid disturbing the root ball as much as possible. If plants are in peat pots, peel away as much of the pot as possible and cover the lip of the pot with soil once it is placed in the earth. Water the new plantings daily for about one week or until new growth appears, then water once or twice a week as needed.

## PROPAGATING

Herbs can be propagated in three ways: from seeds, by division, or from cuttings. Some herbs do not grow quickly or easily from seed, while others, especially hybrids, may produce inferior plants if grown from seeds. In either case, propagating with stem cuttings or by division is a more efficient and effective way of reproducing plants.

To reproduce from cuttings, be sure to take the cuttings from plants in midsummer when plants reach their maturity. Select a stem that has at least six leaves and cut it just above a leaf node. Carefully remove the bottom two or three leaves and any flowers or flower buds, and place the cutting in a small pot or flat in a moistened soilless medium, the same type of material used for growing from seed. Make sure the cutting is inserted deep enough so that the exposed nodes are covered with the medium. Cover the flat or pot with clear plastic or glass and place it in a warm place under bright light. After three or four weeks, you can test to see if the cutting has rooted by gently tugging at the stem. If it has rooted, remove the covering; if not, replace the covering and check in another week. Once the herb has rooted, it can be safely transplanted to the garden.

Propagating by division is a relatively simple process. Most perennial herbs need to be divided every year or two to stimulate growth. Divide herbs in spring when growth starts or in early autumn about six weeks before the first frost.

To divide, dig up the plant, wash the soil from the roots, then carefully pull the roots apart with your hands, and replant the divisions before the roots dry out. If you divide plants in autumn, cut the plants back by half to compensate for the lost roots. Water the divisions well after replanting, then water them daily for about a week.

© Julie O'Neill/Photo/Nats

*Herbs should be watered early in the day so that plants have time to dry thoroughly in the sun.*

## CARING FOR THE HERB GARDEN

Herbs grow easily and, as a result, need only a minimum of encouragement in order to flourish. On the other hand, because herbs are normally bountiful, the garden needs to be tended well so that the plants do not become invasive and scraggly.

A few tips: Herbs grown for their foliage should be pinched to encourage branching and disbudded to produce more abundant and flavorful foliage. Herbs whose stems or roots expand invasively should be controlled by placing a metal edging in the ground to contain roots, or by cultivating them in pots.

The herb garden should be watered at least once a week, although the amount of water a garden needs depends upon the plants and the prevailing weather conditions. For herbs that like dry soil, allow the soil to dry out before watering again; for plants that like extra-moist conditions, keep the soil moist at all times.

When watering, soak plants deeply, and water those with delicate stems from below. Water plants in the morning so that leaves will dry in the sun; leaves left wet overnight are susceptible to disease.

Most herbs do not require intensive fertilization. For annual herbs, the fertilizer put in the soil at planting time is usually sufficient. For perennial herbs, fertilize in the spring. Depending upon the plants and the particular soil conditions, you may wish to fertilize again in midsummer.

Weeds compete with plants for light, water, and nutrients, and often carry diseases and insects. Some plants even create their own weeds by dropping seeds. Keep the garden weed-free and healthy by picking flowers before they turn to seed, and pulling all other weeds when they appear.

Mulch is a protective covering that is spread over the soil and around the bases of plants to keep the ground cool and moist, to prevent weeds from sprouting, and to give the garden a finished look. Organic mulches usually consist of bark chips, leaves or other greenery, and compost; man-made mulch can be made with plastic and newspapers. Again, the kind of mulch you select depends upon the individual variety of the plant and its needs.

### A Word about Garden Pests and Diseases

Because disease, insects, and other pests are so common in the garden, it is useful to become familiar with some of the more common ones and know some of the ways to rid the garden of them. Herbs, due to their fragrance and flavor, tend to ward off many insects and diseases; yet for the same reasons they readily attract certain other pests.

Like all garden plants, herbs may be susceptible to fungi and bacteria that produce leaf spots, wilts, and root rot. Viruses transmitted by aphids and other pests may result in mottled leaves and stunted plant growth. Insects like aphids, leafhoppers, whiteflies, spider mites, beetles, and caterpillars may attack herbs and destroy their leaves and roots. Other pests like grubs, maggot roundworms, snails, and slugs may also feed on herbs—slugs being particularly problematic to herbs.

In general, to avoid pests and diseases, check leaves and stems frequently for off-color or stunted tissue, and remove diseased plants immediately. Always prepare soil properly before planting seeds or plants. Spray plants with water to dislodge insects, other garden pests, and potentially disease-ridden dust and dirt. Allow plants to dry off before nightfall, and make sure air circulates freely around leaves.

You may wish to use an insecticide or a fungicide for particular problems. Recommended pesticides vary from region to

*A parsley worm, one of many pests that may besiege the herb garden.*

© Derek Fell

region, so check with your garden center regarding appropriate use in your area. Also, take special care when using insecticides since you are cultivating edible plants; follow the directions carefully.

### Winterizing

In the fall, carefully clear your garden of all dead matter and debris. Some perennial herbs need mulch during the winter to protect them from cold. Use leaves, evergreen boughs, soil, or man-made materials. Apply the mulch after the ground has frozen and remove it as soon as growth starts in the spring.

30

© Joanne Pavia© Joanne Pavia

# Chapter 2

## GROWING HERBS IN CONTAINERS AND WINDOW BOXES

*Opposite: A small container herb garden designed along a garden wall. Right: Flowering herbs, violas, and pansies growing in a window sill.*

© Anita Sabarese

*Almost any low-growing culinary herb like basil, oregano, marjoram, lavender, chives, thyme, or mint can be grown in a container, a hanging basket, or a window box. In fact, in some cases, they thrive on the individual attention, rather like a spoiled child. In containers, herbs can also be easily moved to collect the best sunlight or to grow more evenly, and, at the same time, serve as attractive decorations on terraces, decks, and windowsills.*

*Select a pot that is in proportion to the size of the mature plant you desire to grow—or conversely, select a plant that is appropriate to the container. In addition, consider the setting in which the container will be placed. Pay special attention to sunlight (herbs need at least 6 hours per day) and wind conditions, especially on high-rise, urban terraces.*

31

© Joanne Pavia

*Thyme, oregano, rosemary, geraniums, and variegated ivy growing side-by-side in attractive pots.*

## CONTAINERS

Containers come in infinite sizes, shapes, and materials. Plastic pots are inexpensive and easy to maintain; unglazed clay pots are more attractive but your herbs will require more attention since water evaporates from clay more easily. Larger, more dramatic-looking containers require special attention since they can become quite heavy and cumbersome when filled with soil. (If you are planning to use extra-large pots, they should be put in position before the herbs are potted.)

Consider using unusual or non-traditional containers for potting herbs. For example, olive oil cans, oriental tea caddies, odd porcelain pieces, tea pots, sugar bowls, or even deep trays make attractive herb containers. Think creatively; some object you may have around the house and are considering tossing out may be ideal for your herbs.

## CULTIVATING THE POTTED HERB

Regardless of your choice of container, all pots need appropriate drainage holes and a layer of gravel, perlite, or broken pottery to prevent water from collecting. For smaller containers, use a soilless mixture of peat moss combined with perlite, vermiculite, or coarse sand. For larger containers, or for herbs that flourish in poor soil, mix garden soil with perlite or vermiculite.

Plants in containers need more frequent watering than those grown in the ground. Check the soil daily, especially if it is unusually hot or the plants are situated on a windy balcony or terrace, and bear in mind the needs of the particular plant. For herbs that like dry soil, water only when the soil is very dry; for those that like moist soil, water the moment the surface of the soil is dry. Potted plants may also need more fertilizer than garden plants, but be careful to not over-fertilize. Pinch leaves often to encourage growth, and if the plant grows unevenly, rotate the container so that it receives light on all sides. Move the plant indoors if there is danger of frost.

Repot plants to a larger container as soon as they show signs of outgrowing their present containers, such as when the roots appear above the soil. As with garden plants, spring is usually the best time to repot.

© Derek Fell

## HANGING BASKETS

For hanging baskets, select herbs whose leaves grow in layers or those that trail. For the most part, avoid plants that tend to grow tall or "upright" unless they are combined with a more horizontal "cousin."

Creeping thyme, ivy, winter savory, rosemary, sage, and some mint all grow well in hanging baskets.

Hanging baskets may need special attention. Some need to be watered more frequently, while others may require more sun or be vulnerable to wind if they are hanging outdoors.

*Some herbs, like parsley, can be grown in hanging baskets.*

*Right: Parsley, thyme, purple sage, and scented geraniums planted together in a windowbox. Below: A variety of herbs, including rosemary, parsley, thyme, basil, and variegated applemint, growing in containers on a brick patio.*

© Joanne Pavia

## WINDOW BOXES

A window box, especially in a sunny kitchen window, can be an ideal place to cultivate a miniature culinary herb garden. Since the space is limited, each herb should be treated individually—and perhaps potted individually. Consider planting parsley, chives, rosemary, thyme, basil, saffron, or even nasturtiums—all of which grow nicely in a small space.

Separate the annual herbs from the perennial herbs. Pot each in separate pots and place the various smaller pots side-by-side in the larger window box.

Many varieties of window boxes are available, from inexpensive, lightweight plastic ones (that tend to crack in cold weather), to clay (which also may crack), to wood. Woodframe window boxes, although sometimes heavy, are attractive and long wearing.

© Derek Fell

# GROWING HERBS INDOORS

Although most herbs are sun-loving, many do grow well when cultivated indoors, particularly chives, dill, chervil, tarragon, mint, basil, oregano, marjoram, parsley, rosemary, and thyme. With such a lavish selection, any cook could happily cultivate a very nice indoor culinary garden.

Culinary herbs grown indoors can be as attractive as they are utilitarian. As with potted outdoor plants, place your herbs in attractive pots, and be creative with your container selections. Since herbs tend to flourish when they are grouped, consider combining them on a tray near a windowsill that not only provides the plants with their needed light, but shows them off to their best advantage.

Pot plants to be grown indoors in the same way you pot them for outdoor containers. Pay special attention to proper drainage. (Consider setting potted herbs in a gravel-lined tray to ensure sufficient drainage.)

As with any potted herb, indoor ones require special care, with regard to watering, lighting, and fertilizing. Pots dry out quickly and should be watered, both top and bottom, frequently—every day in hot weather. In addition to direct watering, sufficient moisture in the atmosphere is also important.

Light is as important as water, and special

*Herbs and salad greens growing on an indoor windowsill.*

© Derek Fell

fluorescent grow lights are available if sunlight is insufficient. Ideally, try to use sunlight during the day and augment with artificial light at night, if necessary. In addition to needing sun, herbs also require relative warmth and should be kept at about a 60 to 70 degrees F (16 to 21 degrees C) temperature when grown indoors.

Indoor herbs also need to be fertilized every three or four weeks in spring and summer and about every six weeks during dormant months. Follow the grower's recommendations carefully.

Indoor herbs may be susceptible to dust and grease, especially if they are grown in the kitchen. Spray or mist the herbs frequently to remove dust, and wipe larger leaves by hand to remove grease. Remove dead or damaged leaves to encourage growth and discourage disease.

# Chapter 3

—

# HARVESTING HERBS

© Amy Reichman/Envision

*One of the great pleasures of growing herbs is that they can be harvested almost immediately. The moment the plants are put into the ground, leaves can be clipped for use in that evening's savory stew. Plus, the garden can be harvested all season long.*

*When harvesting fresh leaves, do not remove more than half the leaves at one time, and do not injure stems. Cut back plants that have grown too tall by midsummer and use their leaves immediately. Or pick leaves before the flowers open when they possess the most flavor, and dry them for later use.*

## DRYING HERBS

The sooner the drying process begins, the better the quality and color of the dried herb. Drying, however, must be gradual, since if herbs are dried too quickly—such as in an oven—essential oils are lost.

For stemmed herbs like sage, thyme, or savory, tie a small bunch of them together with a string, hang them upside down in a well-ventilated place, then remove leaves after they have dried completely. (Drying may take two to three weeks.) If you are drying a small number of leaves, lay the leaves out on muslin, cheesecloth, or brown paper, stretched over a rack so that air circulates evenly. (Drying racks can also be purchased at garden supply centers.)

The recent innovation of drying leaves in a microwave oven works well. Place leaves or stems between two paper towels and set the oven for about $1^{1}/_{2}$ to 2 minutes. Since drying time varies with each herb, do not combine herb varieties in the drying process, and check the herbs frequently.

## HARVESTING SEEDS

Seeds mature a few weeks after flowers fade and should be harvested at that time. Cut stems before the seeds fall and hang them upside down in a dry spot with good air circulation over a clean paper or cloth. You might also place a paper bag or tie a piece of muslin over seed heads to collect the seeds. Seeds dry in about two weeks in a warm, airy place.

*Sunflower seeds, closeup.*

*A nasturtium in bloom, ready to be harvested.*

© Joanne Pavia

## HARVESTING FLOWERS

Edible flowers like nasturtiums should be cut as soon as they are fully open—unless buds are to be used. If not using immediately, put the flowers in water. Remove the stamens, pistils, and the white section at the base of the petals before eating.

Dry flowers in the same manner as you dry leaves. Delicate flowers such as violets or pansies must be spread out carefully to maintain their shape. Allow one to three weeks drying time, and store them flat.

## STORING DRIED HERBS

Store dried leaves, flowers, and seeds in dark, airtight containers. Store leaves and seeds whole to preserve their flavor; crush them just before using. Label bottles with the name of the herb and the date, then store away from heat, moisture, or dust. (Don't store them on a rack over the oven, for example.) Discard dried herbs if they mold or attract insects. Note: The flavor of most herbs deteriorates after a year.

Many herbs can be preserved by infusing them in oil or vinegar. See pages 119–120.

## FREEZING HERBS

Freezing is a very effective method for preserving herbs. Fragile herbs such as basil, chervil, tarragon, fennel, and chives tend to lose their flavor when air dried and should always be frozen. In fact, freezing has become an extremely popular way to preserve all culinary herbs because it is fast, easy, and keeps the herbs fresher and more colorful.

To freeze, simply place the herbs in a plastic bag or plastic container, label, and store in the freezer. Consider making herb blends, like Bouquet Garni (page 115) or an herbes de Provence (page 116) mixture, and freezing them, ready blended.

## Part II

© Steven Mark Needham/Envision

# A CULINARY HERBAL

# Chapter 4

—

# GROWING AND COOKING WITH 32 DELICIOUS HERBS

*Opposite: Fresh tomatoes, peppers, and salad herbs (including parsley, marigold, thyme, sage) arranged in a basket.*

*The following is a list of many of the more common herbs required for a workable kitchen herbal garden, together with growing tips and culinary suggestions. At the end of the herbal is a list of additional herbs one might consider adding or substituting in the garden, depending upon desire and taste.*

*The common, English names of herbs are often as fascinating and evocative as the herbs themselves. For example, shepherd's purse inspires an ancient, rather utilitarian image, while sweet cicely elicits a picture of a gentle loveliness. But common names can vary widely from region to region, and similar names (such as those for many forms of tarragon or mint) can be used for very different plants. (For example, French tarragon has a far sweeter flavor than Russian tarragon.)*

*Fortunately, all plants have a Latin (or scientific) name that is standard around the world. Each Latin name has two parts: the generic name, or genus, and the species. A species of plant is capable of reproducing only with members of that species, but not with other members of its genus. Most genera have many species, for example, the mints (genus: Mentha) have about six hundred species.*

*However, for this culinary herbal, most of the herbs are listed by their common name. The exceptions are certain herbs—for example, the thymes and the mints—that are so similar that many species can be cultivated in more or less the same way in the garden. If, for some reason, you cannot find a particular herb, check the index for the cross-reference.*

**Anise in bloom.**

# Anise / Aniseed

*Pimpinella anisum*
Annual
Height: 12 to 24 inches (30 to 60 cm)

Anise has many medicinal uses, but its spicy, licoricelike flavor has been popular in cooking for centuries. Its dainty white flowers are surprisingly hardy.

### In the Garden
Plant in a sunny place, sheltered from wind, in well-drained soil. Sow seeds in late spring, then thin plants to 6 to 8 inches (15 to 20 cm) apart, but do not transplant. To harvest seeds, cut the plant at ground level, then suspend it upside down until ripe. Pick the leaves from the lower end of the stalk at anytime. Dig up the roots at end of growing season.

### In the Kitchen
Anise seeds are the portion of the plant most frequently used in cooking. Use them whole or crushed in breads, cakes, pies, and confectioneries. Anise seeds also add an interesting tang to vegetables (like carrots) or meats (like Italian sausage). Anise leaves and flowers are tasty in salads, especially fruit salads.

# BASIL

*Ocimum basilicum*
Annual
Height: 15 to 18 inches (38 to 46 cm)

Basil is one of the most esteemed culinary herbs. Because of its warm, spicy flavor it has been used for thousands of years. Along with oregano, basil is almost essential to any Italian dish, especially those containing tomatoes. (Pesto made with basil leaves, is, of course, a classic Italian sauce.) There are many varieties of basil, some with a marvelous lemony fragrance.

### In the Garden

Basil grows best in warm climates, and requires a sunny, warm spot protected from wind, frost, or excessive sun that might scorch the leaves. Sow basil in pots indoors or after the last frost. Plant it in well-drained, moist soil, then thin or transplant to 8 inches (20 cm) apart. Water at midday, not in the evening. To harvest, pick leaves when young.

To preserve, freeze or dry leaves or store whole leaves in olive oil.

### In the Kitchen

Since basil leaves are very delicate, tear rather than chop the leaves. Add them to cooked dishes at the last minute. Basil leaves are also delicious sprinkled over salads and infused in vinegars and oils, particularly olive oil.

*Lettuce-leaf basil.*

45

*Waxy bay laurel leaves.*

# BAY

*Laurus nobilis*
Shrub or evergreen tree
Height: 6 to 12 feet (180 to 360 cm)

Bay, also known as bay laurel, sweet laurel, or sweet bay, has long been associated with ancient Greek and Roman cultures, the laurel wreath symbolizing victory and wisdom. Bay is a large shrub or tree that can be pruned into elegant shapes. The leaves have a pungent aroma. Container-grown bay must be taken inside in winter.

### In the Garden

A bay laurel tree needs full sun, protection from winds, and rich, moist, well-drained soil. To propagate, plant cuttings in a heated propagator with high humidity, then transplant to a frost-free area for the first two years. (Bay laurel is not easy to propagate and it may be easier to buy a plant.) During the summer, keep plants pruned for best growth. Pick leaves anytime; dry leaves to preserve them for cooking.

### In the Kitchen

Bay is one of the classic flavors of French cuisine and is part of a traditional bouquet garni. Bay leaves are often added whole to stews, soups, sauces, marinades, stuffings, and pâtés. Bay leaves are coarse and not easily digestible, so they should always be removed before a dish is served.

# CARAWAY

*Carum carvi*
Hardy biennial
Height: 8 to 24 inches (20 to 60 cm)

Caraway is grown primarily for its seeds, but its leaves and roots are edible and can add an unusual flavor to many dishes. It is not the most attractive garden plant—it flowers only during the first year and gets rangy during the second—but for those who delight in the spicy caraway-seed flavor, it is an interesting choice.

*Caraway leaves.*

### In the Garden

Caraway requires full sun and a rich loamy soil. To propagate, sow seeds in late spring, then thin out or transplant to about 12 inches (30 cm) apart. To harvest, gather leaves when young, and pick seed heads in late summer when seeds are brown. Dig up roots in second year. To collect seeds, hang seed heads upside down over an open counter, or wrap a paper bag around the head.

### In the Kitchen

Caraway seeds have a strong, tart flavor, and are best sprinkled on foods such as beef or pork roasts, cabbage, or rich stews or soups. Caraway seeds also add a piquant flavor to breads, biscuits, and certain pastries such as spicy apple or pear dishes. Young caraway leaves are tasty in salads, and the roots can be cooked and served as a root vegetable instead of potatoes, turnips, or carrots.

# CHERVIL
*Anthriscus cerefolium*
Hardy annual
Height: Approximately 12 inches (30 cm)

Although long a traditional flavoring in French fines herbes, in recent years chervil has become more appreciated in many cuisines—particularly American—for its subtle, parsleylike flavor. Chervil is also a very pretty plant in the garden with its delicate white flowers and lacy leaves. It is relatively easy to grow, and it attains a height of about 12 inches (30 cm).

### In the Garden
Chervil should be planted in light shade, in well-drained soil. Its seeds germinate quickly, and plants should be sown every four to six weeks by scattering them, and then pressing them into the soil. The average garden can have two or three crops per summer. Thin or transplant seedlings to 8 inches (20 cm) apart.

To harvest, gather young leaves. To preserve, freeze or dry, or infuse the leaves in vinegar.

### In the Kitchen
The leaves are most frequently used in cooking, although finely chopped stems can be added with the leaves. In cooked dishes such as soups, stews, and egg dishes, add freshly chopped chervil near the end of the cooking time for the strongest flavor. In addition to its own delicate flavor, chervil also enhances the flavors of other herbs. It is tasty in many foods, especially fish, poultry, and vegetables. Use leaves and stems in salads.

*Lush chervil, a basic herb in French cuisine.*

# CHICORY / SUCCORY

*Cichorium intybus*
Hardy perennial
Height: 2 to 3 feet (60 to 90 cm)

Chicory grows to a height of about 3 feet (90 cm) and produces clear blue flowers, making it a lush and welcome addition to the garden. It comes in several varieties, witloof, which produces chicons or Belgian endives, or magdeburg or brunswick, which produce the roots used to flavor coffee. It is not an easy herb to cultivate, but for some, it may well be worth the effort.

### In the Garden

Chicory grows best in a sunny, open space in light, slightly alkaline soil. To propagate, sow in early summer, then thin or transplant to about 18 inches (46 cm) apart. To grow chicons, dig up roots in autumn, cut leaves to 1 inch (2.5 cm) and trim 1 inch (2.5 cm) off root. Bury the root in sandy compost, water regularly, and chicons—Belgian endive—will be produced in about 4 weeks.

To harvest, gather leaves and flowers when young. Dig up roots for coffee varieties in autumn. To preserve, dry roots and leaves.

*The lovely purple flower of the chicory plant.*

© Dorothy Long/Photo/Nats

### In the Kitchen

To make chicory for use in coffee, dig up the magdeburg or brunswick root, wash it thoroughly, slice it thinly, then dry it in gentle heat. The root can then be roasted and ground.

The chicon or Belgian endive is delicious tossed in salads. Braise it in butter as a vegetable dish or stuff it. Add chicory leaves and flowers to salads.

# CHIVES
*Allium* species
Hardy perennial
Height: 12 to 24 inches (30 to 60 cm)

Allium, or chives, are members of the onion family and include not only the tall green species we normally call chives, but also *A. savtivum*, common garlic. The chives most associated with culinary endeavors include ordinary chives (*A. Schoenoprasum*) with its distinctive and beautiful pink flowers, Chinese chives (*A. tuberosum*), and Welsh onion (*A. fistulosum*).

### In the Garden
Chives are hardy and easy to grow. Plant chives in a sunny area in rich moist soil. Sow seeds in spring, or divide bulbs in autumn or spring, and enrich the soil annually. During the growing season, thin or transplant plants to 9 inches (23 cm) apart and water when dry. To increase the flavor of the leaves and stems, remove flowers. To harvest, cut leaves, leaving 2 inches (5 cm) for regrowth, and pick flowers as they open.

To preserve, freeze or dry chive leaves. The leaves will stay fresh for up to a week if refrigerated in plastic.

© Anita Sabarese

*Flowering chives, a culinary essential.*

### In the Kitchen
Chive leaves, chopped, are used universally as a garnish for soups, sauces, and even as an onion-substitute in some recipes. Use the tasty flowers as a lovely garnish or as a flavoring in vinegar.

# CORIANDER

*Coriandrum sativum*
Annual
Height: 18 to 24 inches (46 to 60 cm)

Coriander, also known as Chinese parsley or cilantro, is best known as a signature ingredient in many ethnic cuisines, including Chinese, Indian, Mexican, and Scandinavian. The plant has a unique sweet/savory fragrance and flavor, and the seeds have a lemony flavor.

## *In the Garden*

Coriander requires full sun and rich, light soil. To propagate, sow in autumn in mild climates or early spring in colder ones, then thin or transplant plants to 8 to 12 inches (20 to 30 cm) apart. Like dill, coriander should be planted away from fennel since fennel adversely affects the flavor of it. To harvest, pick young leaves anytime. Collect seeds when brown, but before they drop. Dig up roots in autumn. Leaves can be dried or frozen; seeds can be dried.

## *In the Kitchen*

Coriander leaves are frequently used in Oriental stir-fries, Indian curries and chutneys, and Mexican chili dishes, dips, and sauces. The leaves have a pungent flavor that mingles well in certain breads, biscuits, and pastries and is delicious added to most soups and vegetable dishes. Also, add seeds and stems to curries, soups, and stews. The root is also edible as a vegetable, or can be grated into various savory dishes.

*Pungent coriander is an important ingredient in many exotic cuisines.*

# DILL

*Anethum graveolens*
Hardy annual
Height: 2 to 4 feet (60 to 120 cm)

Dill, one of the most universal culinary plants, is found in many European cuisines. This tall, airy-looking plant is found in virtually any herb garden. Its feathery leaves, yellow, umbrellalike flower, and seeds are all used in cooking to add a distinctive flavor to many dishes—particularly fish, vegetables, and sauces.

*Dill, a necessity in the garden and in the kitchen.*

### In the Garden

Although dill is hardy and relatively easy to cultivate, it requires full sun and protection from wind. Sow seeds from spring until midsummer in rich, well-drained soil, and thin or transplant back to 12 inches (20 cm) apart. Do not plant dill and fennel close together; they cross-pollinate, which dulls their flavors.

Leaves can be picked at anytime, but flowers are best when the fruits begin to form. To collect seeds, hang the whole plant over a cloth after the flower turns brown. Freeze or dry dill leaves and dry the seeds.

### In the Kitchen

Carefully chop dill leaves. They are delicious in many savory dishes like soups and cream sauces. Potatoes with dill is classic, and fish is often well enhanced with dill leaves. The threadlike texture of the leaves provides an attractive appearance as well as a savory flavor.

Use dill seeds whole or ground in vinegars and pickled vegetables. They are delicious cooked with vegetables and breads, and in some sweet/savory pastries.

The flowering top can be added to dill-flavored vinegar (with seeds) or to pickled vegetables.

# FENNEL

*Foeniculum vulgare*
Perennial
Height: 5 to 7 feet (150 to 210 cm)

Fennel is one of the oldest cultivated plants in history, probably because virtually every part of the plant—seed, leaves, stems, bulbs—is edible. There are several varieties of fennel including sweet fennel, which is used primarily for its fine leaves, and Florence fennel or finocchio, which produces the licorice-flavored bulbs.

### In the Garden
Fennel requires full sun and well-drained loamy soil. To propagate, sow seeds in late spring; divide plants in autumn. While growing, plants should be thinned or transplanted to about 2 feet (60 cm) apart. Do not grow near dill or coriander as the seeds will cross-pollinate.

To harvest fennel, pick young stems and leaves as required; collect ripe seeds; and dig up bulbs in autumn. Fennel leaves do not dry well, so to preserve, freeze the stems and leaves or infuse them in oil or vinegar. Seeds can be dried.

© Anita Sabarese

*With fennel, every part of the plant is useful.*

### In the Kitchen
Fennel seeds add a delicious aniselike taste to sauces, fish, sausages, and certain baked goods such as breads, rolls, and savory pastries. Leaves are tasty in salads, soups, and stuffings. Eat the bulbs from Florence fennel (finocchio) cooked as a vegetable or raw as a crudité or in salads.

# HORSERADISH

*Armoracia rusticana*
Hardy perennial
Height: 18 to 24 inches (45 to 60 cm)

Horseradish is very easy to grow, but the stems and leaves are not pretty and its roots can become so tenacious that they are difficult to eradicate. But for the serious gardener, horseradish can be an interesting addition to a kitchen garden. In Germany and certain Scandinavian countries, horseradish has been used to flavor fish sauces, but it is most famous as the accompaniment to classic British roast beef. The leaves are occasionally used in salads.

### In the Garden

Plant horseradish in a sunny spot in rich, moist soil. To propagate, sow seeds in early spring, or divide roots or take root cuttings. Plant roots vertically at a depth of about 2 inches (5 cm). Thin or transplant to 12 inches (20 cm) apart.

To harvest, dig up roots as needed or in autumn; pick young leaves. To preserve, store roots in sand, or immerse whole washed roots in white wine vinegar. Leaves can be dried.

© Anita Sabarese

### In the Kitchen

In cooking, the horseradish root is the part of the plant that is most well known. It can be grated into salads, sauces, mayonnaise, or fillings. Horseradish sauce—made with whipped cream or sour cream—goes well with roast beef and is also tasty with flavorful fish.

*The hardy horseradish.*

# HYSSOP

*Hyssopus offinalis*
Perennial
Height: 18 to 24 inches (45 to 60 cm)

Hyssop is most well known as a medicinal herb. Ancient peoples used it to relieve colds and sore throats, and modern scientists use the mold that grows on the leaves to produce penicillin. In the kitchen, it is used to flavor wines and teas, and for centuries it has been employed by the Benedictine monks for flavoring their liqueurs. With its beautiful purple flower it makes an attractive addition to the herb garden, especially in hedging and borders.

### In the Garden
Hyssop needs full sun and light, well-drained soil. Sow seeds or divide roots in spring, then transplant or thin to 24 inches (60 cm) apart. Hyssop can grow to up to 24 inches (60 cm) in height, but should be cut back to about 10 to 12 inches (25 to 30 cm). To harvest, pick flowers and tops as flowering begins, and gather leaves anytime. To preserve, dry young leaves and flowering tops.

© Joanne Pavia

*Hyssop, as elegant as it is useful.*

### In the Kitchen
Use hyssop leaves, which are pungent and aromatic, in small amounts in game and fish dishes, soups and stews, and even in fruit compotes or savory pies. Add the flowers to salads. Hyssop leaves make a soothing tea and an interesting flavoring when added to liquors.

# LAVENDER

*Lavandula angustifolia (L. officinalis or L. spica)*
Evergreen shrub
Height: 2 to 6 inches (5 to 15 cm)

One of the most romantic sights in the world is a shimmering field of lavender as it grows in Provence, France. Lavender comes in more than ten species that vary in color from white to pink to purple, but all of them produce small, highly scented flowers that grow in spikes, 2 to 6 inches (5 to 15 cm) long. One of the world's classic fragrances, lavender is also known for its medicinal properties. However, not only is it beautiful in the garden, it can add elegance to many dishes in the kitchen.

### In the Garden

Lavender should be grown in a sunny open space in well-drained, sandy, slightly alkaline soil. To propagate, take stem cuttings in spring or divide; sow fresh seeds in late summer or autumn. Thin or transplant to 12 inches (20 cm) apart. To harvest, gather flowering stems as the flowers open; pick leaves anytime. To preserve lavender, dry the stems by laying on open trays or hanging in small bunches.

© Jerry Pavia

*Lavender, the most romantic herb.*

### In the Kitchen

Lavender flowers are flavorful in jams and vinegars, or mixed with savory herbs for soups and stews. The flowers can also be crystalized and used to garnish ice cream, cakes, cookies, and other confectioneries. Although lavender leaves are bitter, they can be used in very small amounts in some dishes like salads.

56

# LEMON BALM / MELISSA

*Melissa offinalis*
Perennial
Height: Approximately 3 feet (90 cm)

Lemon balm is a pretty, bushy plant with white summer flowers and lemon-scented leaves. Considered a sacred plant by the Greeks, it was long valued for its medicinal uses, particularly in dispelling melancholy and depression. It is a valuable and attractive garden plant, and its leaves provide a sharp, refreshing flavor to many dishes.

### In the Garden
Lemon balm requires full sun with some shade and moist soil. Sow, divide plants, or take stem cuttings in spring. Thin or transplant to 18 inches (45 cm) apart. After plants have flowered, prune them back in order to hold their shape. To harvest, pick leaves anytime, but flavor is best once flowers open. Dry leaves by cutting stems to the ground and hanging them upside down or preserve fresh leaves in vinegar.

### In the Kitchen
Lemon balm leaves mingle well with other herbs and add a refreshing lemon taste to salads, fruits, teas, and fish, poultry, and pork dishes. Lemon balm is also a nice herb to add to multiherbed vinegars.

*Lemon balm not only produces attractive leaves, but its white flowers are equally lovely.*

*Lemon verbena, a small elegant plant with a clean, lemony fragrance.*

# LEMON VERBENA
*Aloysia triphylla*
Shrub
Height: 15 to 18 inches (38 to 45 cm)

The lemon verbena is a small, delicate shrub that grows best in warm climates. It is a native of South America, brought to Europe in the sixteenth century and used to scent oils with its clean, lemony fragrance. Today it is used primarily as a garnish, not only because the leaves are attractive but because of their sharp, lemon flavor.

### In the Garden
The lemon verbena shrub requires full sun and well-drained alkaline soil for growth and much shelter to survive the winter frost. Sow seeds in spring, or grow from cuttings taken in late spring. Thin or transplant bushes to 3 feet (90 cm) apart, and prune branches for new growth. Leaves can be picked anytime, but are best when the delicate white or purple flowers are blooming. Dry or infuse leaves in oil or vinegar.

### In the Kitchen
Lemon verbena leaves make a very special garnish on cakes, fresh fruit, or ice cream dishes, or finely chop the leaves and add to sweet drinks and teas, fruit puddings, and homemade jellies. Basically, lemon verbena leaves can be used in any dish requiring a strong lemon flavor or scent.

# LOVAGE
*Levisticum officinale*
Perennial
Height: Approximately 3 feet (90 cm)

Sometimes known by the appealing name love parsley, lovage actually has a flavor more like celery. It is a grand plant, tall, handsome, with a strong savory flavor. Lovage is a fine addition to the garden—and to the table.

### In the Garden
Lovage needs full sun or partial shade and grows well in rich, moist, well-drained soil. (Lovage thrives in colder climates.) To propagate, sow seeds in late summer, or take root cuttings with buds in late spring or autumn. In spring, put in new plants or thin or transplant older plants 2 to 3 feet (60 to 90 cm) apart. To harvest, pick leaves as needed and gather seeds when ripe. To preserve, freeze or dry leaves, and dry seeds and roots.

### In the Kitchen
Lovage is most commonly used for its leaves, which are delicious in soups, stews, stocks, or salads—they can even be stuffed. Lovage seeds are traditionally added to liqueurs and cordials, but are also tasty in breads, rice, salads, or potatoes as a change from dill or parsley. Stems can be steamed; roots can be cooked and eaten.

*Lovage leaves add a pungent, celery-like flavor to soups and stews.*

# MARJORAM

*Origanum majorana*
Perennial
Height: 6 to 20 inches (15 to 50 cm)

Marjoram, or sweet marjoram, part of the oregano family, is one of the more popular culinary herbs. It is a small plant, grows easily in the garden, and has a sweet scent and a spicy flavor, long associated with many Mediterranean cuisines.

### In the Garden
Marjoram should be planted in full sun with some shade, in well-drained, dry, alkaline soil. Marjoram tends to have a stronger flavor when grown in rich soil. Sow seeds indoors in spring, and plant seedlings about 8 inches (20 cm) apart. Then fertilize. Divide plants in spring or autumn; take root or stem cuttings from late spring to midsummer. Thin out or transplant to 12 to 18 inches (30 to 45 cm), and prune back plants before they die. To harvest, pick young leaves anytime; to preserve, freeze or dry leaves.

© Derek Fell

### In the Kitchen
Sweet marjoram leaves have a distinctive sweet-and-spicy flavor. Use them to make an aromatic tea or add them to salads. Use the leaves as a flavoring to Italian foods, vegetables, stuffings and fish, poultry, and meat dishes. Sweet marjoram is also used in Greek, Moroccan, and other Mediterranean cuisines.

*Wild marjoram is one of the most popular culinary herbs.*

# MINTS

*Mentha* species
Hardy perennial
Height: 1½ inches to 3 feet (4 to 90 cm)

Traditionally a symbol of hospitality, mint comes in over 600 varieties and is one of the most popular herbs for the culinary garden. (For culinary uses, consider spearmint, crinkle-leaved black peppermint, applemint, English pennyroyal, or lemon mint.) It is an attractive plant for the garden, and an extremely useful and flavorful plant in the kitchen.

### In the Garden

Mints can grow in sun or partial shade and require moist, well-drained, nutrient-rich, alkaline soil. To propagate, take root or stem cuttings or divide in spring and autumn, or sow seeds in spring. Thin or transplant to 9 to 12 inches (23 to 30 cm) apart, and remove all flowering stems to avoid cross-pollination between species. Mint often grows best in pots because the roots grow wildly and tend to invade other plants. To harvest, pick leaves just before flowering. To preserve, dry or freeze the leaves, or infuse them in oil or vinegar.

### In the Kitchen

Mints are remarkably versatile herbs. Spearmint and peppermint make invigorating teas, and are delicious in sauces, vinegars, and syrups—especially when combined with chocolate. Mint leaves are also delicious crystallized in sugar and used for decoration on cakes, cookies, and other confectioneries.

Although mint is normally associated with sweet flavors, the leaves add a fresh flavor to vegetables, potatoes, rice, stuffings, and even certain stews and soups. Many Middle Eastern and Mediterranean cuisines sprinkle mint over grilled meats and other savory dishes.

*Mint comes in over 600 varieties. Among those most useful in the kitchen are peppermint (above left), and spearmint (above right).*

© Mike Magnuson

*Nasturtiums are grown for both decoration and consumption.*

## NASTURTIUM

*Tropaeolum majus*
Annual
Height: Approximately 12 inches (30 cm)

Nasturtiums are grown both as flowers and as herbs. They come in various colors—red, orange, and yellow—have rounded leaves, and make a bright addition to the garden. The peppery-flavored flowers, buds, and leaves add a piquant taste to salads.

### In the Garden
Nasturtiums require sunny placement and light, somewhat dry, well-drained soil. Sow seeds in spring after the last frost about 8 to 12 inches (20 to 30 cm) apart. To harvest, pick stems at ground level, and use the leaves, buds, and flowers when fresh.

### In the Kitchen
Nasturtium adds a zesty, peppery flavor to salads, to fruit, egg, and pasta dishes, and to light stews, sauces, and soups. Nasturtium's attractive flowers and leaves also make lovely garnishes.

# OREGANO

*Origanum* species
Perennial
Height: 8 to 24 inches ( 20 to 60 cm)

Oregano comes in a number of varieties—including Italian oregano and Greek oregano (very flavorful), and is even sometimes confused with marjoram. It is often included in a bouquet garni, especially for dishes native to southern France and other Mediterranean cultures. Nevertheless, despite the confusion, it is one of the most important culinary herbs.

### In the Garden
Oregano grows best in full sun in light, well-drained, alkaline soil. To propagate, sow seeds in spring and plant seedlings about 12 inches (20 cm) apart in late spring. Divide plants in spring, or take stem cuttings. To harvest, cut leaves anytime. To preserve, hang stems upside down to dry, and then separate leaves.

### In the Kitchen
Oregano has distinctive peppery- or savory-flavored leaves. The leaves can be chopped and blended with spicy foods such as pizza, egg and cheese dishes, grilled meats, and spicy sauces and stews. Oregano combines well with certain other herbs—like garlic.

*Oregano comes in many varieties, and is an important herb in many Mediterranean cuisines.*

# PARSLEY

*Petroselinum crispum*
Hardy biennial
Height: 12 to 18 inches (30 to 45 cm)

Like several other popular culinary herbs, parsley boasts many varieties, but curled parsley and Italian parsley are those most commonly associated with cooking. All parsleys are rich in vitamins, minerals, and chlorophyll (which serves to cleanse the digestive system) and are attractive as a garnishing herb. Also, parsley is an ingredient in a classic bouquet garni.

### In the Garden

Parsley requires full sun or light shade and rich, moist soil. If grown from seed, sow from spring to late summer; however, parsley is slow to germinate so purchased plants often prove more productive. Thin or transplant to 9 to 12 inches (23 to 30 cm) apart. Protect in cold weather or take indoors where it flourishes.

To harvest, cut leaves with a scissors. (They are best during the first year.) Dig up roots in autumn of second year. Dry or freeze leaves.

© Robert E. Lyons/Photo/Nats

### In the Kitchen

Add raw parsley leaves to salads. To preserve its flavor in cooking, chop and add at the end. Parsley mingles well with egg and vegetable dishes, and particularly with potatoes, soups, stews, sauces, and light fish dishes. Both curly parsley and Italian parsley are perfect as garnishes.

*"Extra-curled dwarf" parsley, one of the most popular culinary herbs.*

# ROSEMARY

*Rosmarinus officinalis*
Tender evergreen perennial
Height: 3 to 5 feet (90 to 150 cm)

Rosemary is a summer herb garden classic, and a basic herb to any kitchen. In the garden, it is classified as a perennial, but because it is such a tender plant, it is often grown as an annual, and its 3- to 5-foot (90- to 150-cm) plantings make an interesting hedge or border plant. When grown as a perennial, it blooms with pale blue flowers. Like several other popular herbs, such as thyme and mint, rosemary has several varieties. Its subtle flavor mingles well with other herbs and enhances many foods.

### In the Garden
Rosemary requires full sun and protection from cold winds, as well as rich, well-drained, slightly moist soil. Sow under heat in spring or outdoors in summer, although rosemary propagates best by cuttings. Transplant when large enough to handle with 2 to 3 feet (60 to 90 cm) between plants. To harvest, pick small leaves anytime. To preserve, dry sprigs and branches, and then strip off the needlelike leaves before storing.

© Robert E. Lyons/Photo/Nats

*Tender rosemary, as classic in the herb garden as it is in the kitchen.*

### In the Kitchen
Use rosemary leaves to flavor virtually any dish, from grilled meats—especially lamb and pork—to chicken, fish, potatoes, vegetables, and even fresh fruits.

## SAGE
*Salvia officinalis*
Perennial
Height: 1 to 3 feet (30 to 90 cm)

Sage is an ancient and classic herb, most frequently used today in stuffings, stews, and sausages. It comes in several varieties, including a pineapple-scented sage, which is native to warm climates. With its low, broad leaves, it is an attractive plant for the garden, and with its unique flavor, a welcome addition to the kitchen.

### In the Garden
Sage requires full sun or light shade and sandy, well-drained soil. Plant seedlings in early spring, and keep plants about 18 inches (45 cm) apart. To harvest, pick leaves before the plant blooms in spring and again in late summer. To preserve, dry the leaves.

### In the Kitchen
Hardy, flavorful sage leaves combine best with rich meats such as pork, beef, or game, and help in digestion. Sage also is delicious in certain cheese dishes, and makes an interesting herbed-infused vinegar.

© Derek Fell

*Sage is a particularly attractive herb in the garden, and adds a strong and pungent flavor to pork, beef, or game.*

# SORREL (GARDEN)

*Rumex acetosa*
Perennial
Height: 6 to 18 inches (15 to 45 cm)

Sorrel is a rich-looking plant, used widely in French cooking. Its spinachlike leaves have a sharp, lemony flavor, and spice up a number of classic dishes.

### In the Garden

Sorrel is a hardy plant and relatively easy to grow. It requires rich, well-drained soil and full sun. Sow seeds or plant seedlings in early spring or fall, cut plants back during the growing season to encourage tender leaves, and water frequently. To harvest, pick leaves anytime and use them fresh.

### In the Kitchen

In French cooking, sorrel serves as the basis for many sauces, especially fish and egg sauces, and, of course, classic sorrel soup. It blends well with spinach and is an interesting addition to salads and cooked vegetables.

*French sorrel leaves have a sharp, lemony flavor.*

# SUNFLOWER

*Helianthus* species
Annual
Height: 4 to 10 inches (120 to 300 cm)

Sunflowers are perhaps the largest herb. Cultivated for seeds (*Helianthus annuus*) or for their delicious tubers (*Helianthus tuberosus*), sunflowers are a dramatic and interesting addition to any garden. (Leaves and flower buds can also be added to salads.) Sunflowers are native to North America; the Native Americans originally cultivated them. Their large daisylike yellow flower has long served as a symbol of the sun.

### In the Garden
Sunflowers need full sun and well-drained loamy soil. Sow seeds in their shells in spring, then transplant to 12 to 18 inches (30 to 45 cm) apart for best growth. To harvest, pick leaves and flower buds as required. To collect seeds, cut flower heads and hang upside down until seeds fall or cover the head with a paper bag. Gather tuberous roots in autumn. To preserve, dry seeds and store tubers in a cool place.

### In the Kitchen
Sunflower seeds are nutritious—for birds as well as humans. Eat seeds raw or roasted in their shells, and add seeds and raw flower buds to salads.

The tuberous roots of one variety of sunflower are known as Jerusalem artichokes, although they are neither from Jerusalem nor in any way related to artichokes. Cook and serve them as a vegetable, or grated and added to salads.

*Face to face with a giant sunflower.*

# SWEET CICELY

*Myrrhis odorata*
Hardy perennial
Height: 2½ to 3 feet (75 to 90 cm)

Sweet cicely—also known as sweet chervil and British myrrh—is a hardy perennial plant whose leaves have an aniselike flavor. Its stems, seedpods, and roots are also edible, and the seeds have a subtle nutty flavor. It bears attractive flowers and has a sweet woodland scent making it an attractive garden plant. With its multifaceted culinary aspects, it is also valuable in the kitchen.

### In the Garden

Sweet cicely requires light shade and rich soil. Sow seeds indoors in autumn as the seed requires several months of cold winter in order to germinate. Plant seedlings 18 to 24 inches (40 to 60 cm) apart; try to avoid transplanting. To harvest, pick young leaves any time, collect unripe seeds when green, and dig up roots in autumn. To preserve, dry unripe seeds; clean and peel root and infuse it in wine or brandy. The leaves do not dry well, but can be frozen.

© Anita Sabarese

*Sweet cicely bears a dainty flower, a pleasant woodland scent, and a mild, anise flavor.*

### In the Kitchen

Sweet cicely leaves are delicious in soups, stews, teas, and fruit dishes. The seeds have a sweet, nutty flavor and are delicious in fruit salads, fruit pies, and even in ice cream. The leaves are also particularly good in salad dressings and omelettes, and the root can be grated raw into salad dressing or salads.

© Derek Fell

*Often grown as part of an English country garden, the leaves of sweet rocket add a tangy flavor to salads.*

# SWEET ROCKET

*Hesperis matronalis*
Hardy biennial
Height: 3 to 4 feet (90 to 120 cm)

Although sweet rocket is a native of Italy, it is also traditionally associated with an English cottage garden, with its lovely, innocent purple-pink flower. Its leaves and flowers add an elegant and tangy flavor to salads and fruit dishes.

### In the Garden

Sweet rocket requires light shade and rich, loamy, well-drained soil. To propagate, sow seeds or plant seedlings in late spring; thin seedlings or transplant in autumn to about 18 inches (45 cm) apart. To harvest, gather leaves, flowers, or seedpods at anytime. Leaves can be dried.

### In the Kitchen

Add sweet rocket flowers to salads, fruit dishes, or use it as an elegant garnish for ice creams, cakes, or other confectioneries. Chop or crush leaves and use in salads, soups, and stews. Sweet rocket is related to the mustard family and has a similar flavor.

# SWEET WOODRUFF

*Galium odoratum*
Perennial
Height: 10 to 15 inches (25 to 38 cm)

Sweet woodruff evokes images of medieval English knights on steeds and ladies waiting to be saved. Due to its delectable fragrance when dried (like new-mown hay), it has been used to scent linens, pillows, and clothing—and, indeed, rooms—for centuries. Hung in garlands, strewn on floors, sprinkled in linen, and stuffed in mattresses, it prevented musty—and other—odors. It has also long been used to flavor May wine. An attractive garden plant, it is also a nice multifaceted addition to a culinary garden.

### In the Garden
Sweet woodruff flourishes in semishade and grows well under trees in moist, loamy soil. To propagate, sow seeds in late summer in moist shaded soil, or divide the creeping root after flowering is finished. Transplant plants in the spring to about 12 inches (30 cm) apart. Pick leaves and flowering stems anytime. To preserve, dry leaves and store whole to preserve their scent.

### In the Kitchen
Although sweet woodruff is best known for its fragrance, it is flavorful in teas and is the classic ingredient in May wine punches.

*Sweet woodruff is a beautiful addition to the garden and is the signature flavoring for classic May Wine.*

71

© Derek Fell

*Tarragon is one of the most important culinary herbs, especially in classic French cooking.*

# TARRAGON
*Artemisia dracunculus*
Hardy perennial
Height: 2 to 3 feet (60 to 90 cm)

Tarragon is one of the most important culinary herbs, and together with chervil and parsley forms the basis for French fines herbes—and thus many fine, French dishes. Tarragon has several varieties, but one of the most common is French tarragon, which has a refined, almost sweet flavor.

### In the Garden
Tarragon requires a relatively sunny spot, sheltered from wind, and rich, light, dry soil. Tarragon must be grown from divisions or cuttings. Divide roots in spring, or take cuttings in summer, and thin or transplant to about 24 inches (60 cm) apart. Cut back in the fall and protect with straw in the winter.

To harvest, pick leaves at anytime. Dry, freeze, or infuse them in vinegar or oil.

### In the Kitchen
Tarragon leaves provide a subtle sweet/savory fragrance and aroma to many dishes from soups and stews, to chicken, fish, and game dishes. Tarragon is not normally used for grilled or roasted meats, but it can provide a special flavor there too. It is a stunning ingredient in many sauces, béarnaise sauce being the most well known.

# THYMES
*Thymus* species
Perennial
Height: 3 to 18 inches (8 to 45 cm)

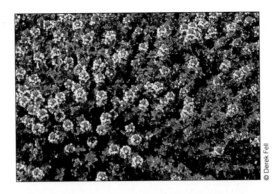

*Thyme comes in more than 100 varieties, including common kitchen thyme (top) or lemon thyme (bottom).*

Thyme is one of the most ubiquitous herbal plants, boasting more than one hundred species and varieties, including *Thymus vulgaris*, common kitchen thyme, and lemon thyme (*Thymus* x *citriodorus*), a cousin that makes a delicious herbal tea. Even bees make a honey from thyme, and the ancient Scots made a thyme tea that inspired courage. Thyme grows from 3 to 12 inches (8 to 20 cm) in height, provides an aromatic addition to the garden, and is indispensible in the kitchen.

### In the Garden
Thyme needs full sun and light, dry, well-drained soil. To propagate, start plants indoors and set them in spring spaced about 12 inches (20 cm) apart. To grow, thin or transplant if necessary to 9 to 15 inches (23 to 38 cm), and prune frequently in summer. Thyme leaves dry or freeze well, but can also be infused in vinegar or oil.

### In the Kitchen
Thyme is part of the classic bouquet garni, together with parsley and bay. It is an essential herb to any cook—particularly the French cook—and is a basic ingredient in many stocks, marinades, stuffings, sauces, and soups. With its pungent flavor, thyme is a delicious addition to poultry, fish, shellfish, vegetable, and game dishes.

# WILD CELERY

*Apium graveolens*
Hardy biennial
Height: 1 to 3 feet (30 to 90 cm)

Wild celery or smallage is one of the less-common culinary herbs, but it adds a celerylike flavor to soups, stews, and vegetables. With its tall stems, yellow-white flowers (which are produced during the second year), it is an interesting addition to the garden.

### In the Garden

Plant wild celery in a sunny area, away from cool winds, in rich, moist, well-drained soil. To propagate, sow under heat indoors in early spring or outdoors in late spring, and transplant or thin to about 18 inches (45 cm) apart at end of first summer. To harvest, pick leaves in late summer, and collect seeds when they are ripe. Dry, freeze, or infuse in vinegar.

### In the Kitchen

Add wild celery seeds to soups, stews, and casseroles or use for pickling. Wild celery seeds can also be an ingredient in celery salt, or used freshly ground as a salt substitute.

The leaves, especially when dried, have a stronger flavor than ordinary celery, but can be used to flavor the same sorts of dishes, including fish or chicken stocks, salads, cheese dishes, poultry, fish, or shellfish.

© Anita Sabarese

*Wild celery or smallage is a bit more difficult to cultivate, but adds interest to both the garden and various spicy dishes.*

74

# WILD STRAWBERRY

*Fragaria vesca*
Hardy evergreen
Height: 10 to 12 inches (25 to 30 cm)

Growing wild strawberries in the common kitchen garden is relatively unusual, but they are so delectable, they are worth the time and trouble. Wild strawberries are less sweet than cultivated strawberries but they are no less delicious.

### In the Garden

Plant wild strawberries in a cool, sheltered area in well-drained alkaline soil. Sow seeds in spring; then transplant or thin to 12 inches (30 cm) apart. Pick fruit as it ripens, and collect leaves as required. To preserve, freeze or bottle the fruit, and dry the leaves.

### In the Kitchen

Strawberries are best eaten freshly picked with cream. However, if there are any left over, they can be made into jams, jellies, syrups, liqueurs, cordials, and any number of pastries.

Strawberry leaves have a bite to them. Use them to flavor stocks or combine with other herbs to add a tangy flavor to salads.

© Philip Beaurune/Photo/Nats

*Wild strawberries are among the most beautiful plants in the herb garden.*

75

*Many less-common herbs are delightful additions to the culinary herb garden, including comfrey (top), borage (bottom left), and tansy (bottom right).*

## ADDITIONAL SUGGESTIONS

The following herbs are also excellent additions to a kitchen garden, depending on your taste: angelica, borage, mustard, chamomile, costmary, meadowsweet, curry plant, salad burnet, cowslip, garden rue, winter savory, comfrey, tansy, fenugreek, winter purslane, and summer purslane. You will find basic growing instructions on seed packages.

© Joanne Pavia

## THE HERBAL SALAD BOWL

Since so many herbs taste delicious in salads or salad dressings, many gardeners include lettuces and salad greens in their herb gardens. Follow seed packet directions for growing and cultivating lettuces. Following are a few possibilities: arugula, garden cress, romaine lettuce, Boston lettuce, watercress, butterhead lettuce, leaf lettuce, and radicchio.

*Top: Pansies are among the prettiest edible flowers, adding color to the garden and the table. Bottom: Various lettuces can easily be included in the herb garden, including leaf lettuce, chicory, and radicchio.*

## EDIBLE FLOWERS

Edible flowers not only make colorful and fragrant additions to an herb garden, they provide numerous creative possibilities for the cook. Edible flowers can be added raw to salad, dried, infused in oil, or used as a garnish on meat dishes, pastas, and desserts. The following are some of the most popular: sweet violet, marigold, clove pink, evening primrose, poppy, scented geranium, French marigold, pansy, rose, daisy, and nasturtium.

Remember: Most flowers are not edible—in fact, some can be poisonous.

© Envision

# — *Part III* —

Steven Mark Needham/Envision

# HERBS IN THE KITCHEN

# Chapter 5

---

# COOKING WITH HERBS

**Opposite: A delectable flatbread seasoned with whole sage leaves.**

*Herbs, when used with care and grace, turn any simple dish into something subtly magnificent. What's more, while many herbs provide added fragrance, flavor, and texture to a dish, some even aid digestion.*

*The fifty recipes included here are meant to provide an overall feel for cooking with herbs. Basic recipes for such dishes as omelettes, fish, chicken, and vegetables have been included with suggestions for substitutions. Also, recipes for infused vinegars and oils and herbal butters and teas are also here to show a variety of ways to use herbs.*

*Most of the recipes call for fresh herbs, but in most cases, dried or frozen herbs could be substituted. (As a rule of thumb and flavor, one teaspoon of dried herbs is equal to one tablespoon of fresh herbs; or, to put it another way, to substitute dried herbs for fresh, cut the amount by one third.)*

*Try to pick herbs from the garden as close to mealtime as possible. If fresh herbs are stored before using, they should be stored in a plastic bag in the refrigerator. Herbs are delicate and should be added to cooked dishes as late as possible in the cooking process, unless otherwise instructed in the recipe.*

*Cooking with herbs—especially those grown in one's own garden—is one of life's greatest pleasures.*

*Opposite: Greek olives and marinated chèvre are elegant yet simple hors d'oeuvres.*

## Greek Olives with Herbs

Makes 2 cups

These olives make an elegant hors d'oeuvre and, left in their oil, stay delicious for months.

*2 cups (1 pint) Calamata olives, pitted*
*1 bay leaf*
*2 teaspoons chopped fresh rosemary*
*1 teaspoon chopped fresh mint*
*2 teaspoons lemon rind, minced*
*About ½ cup high-quality olive oil*

Drain liquid from the olives and reserve. Into a 1-pint canning jar, place the olives, bay leaf, rosemary, mint, and lemon rind. Add olive oil and enough reserved liquid to cover the olives. Shake the jar to distribute the herbs evenly, then allow the olives to marinate in the oil for 2 or 3 days before serving. Refrigerate.

## Marinated Chèvre with Herbs

Makes 2 or 3 crotins, or 2 rolls

Marinated chèvre served with crisp crackers, such as Carr's Water Biscuits, is a simple and tasty hors d'oeuvre.

*2 or 3 small rounds of goat's-milk cheese or*
*    1 goat's-milk cheese roll cut in half*
*1 to 2 tablespoons herbes de Provence (see page 116)*
*2 teaspoons coarsely ground black pepper*
*1 or 2 whole cloves garlic, peeled*
*About 1 cup high-quality imported olive oil*

Sprinkle the cheese with the herbs and black pepper. Place the cheese in a 1-pint, wide-mouthed canning jar. Add the garlic and pour on the oil to cover. The cheese will keep for a month, and will become more flavorful the longer it remains in the oil. Refrigerate.

© Michael Grand

© Steven Mark Needham/Envision

*Deviled Eggs are perfect for summer picnics.*

## Old-Fashioned Deviled Eggs with Dill

Makes 12 stuffed eggs

*6 large eggs*
*¼ cup mayonnaise*
*2 tablespoons grainy mustard*
*5 tablespoons chopped fresh dill*
*Salt and freshly ground pepper*
*Whole sprigs of dill for garnish*

Place the eggs in rapidly boiling water and boil for 10 to 12 minutes. Remove from heat and let stand for 17 to 20 minutes. When eggs are hard-cooked, immediately run them under cold water, then allow them to cool completely.

Peel the eggs, slice them in half, and empty the yolks into a bowl. Mash the yolks, then add the mayonnaise, mustard, dill, and salt and pepper to taste.

Arrange the whites on a serving platter. Spoon 1 or 2 tablespoons of the yolk mixture into the whites. Garnish with a small sprig of dill. Serve chilled.

## Katherine's Old-Fashioned Cream of Tomato Soup

*Makes 6 cups*

My great-aunt Katherine taught English literature at Case Western Reserve University in Ohio, but during the summer months, she retired to her family home in upstate New York and spent many hours tending her garden. As a child, I would often visit her during the last week of my summer vacation and, invariably, she would make the following tomato soup from beautiful tomatoes picked fresh from her garden.

*2 cups fresh tomatoes, peeled and chopped*
*½ cup chopped celery*
*¼ cup chopped onion*
*1 tablespoon sugar*
*8 tablespoons (1 stick) butter*
*½ cup all-purpose flour*
*4 cups heavy cream*
*Salt and freshly ground black pepper to taste*
*¼ cup chopped fresh tarragon*

In a saucepan, place the tomatoes, celery, onion, and sugar, and simmer for about 15 minutes until the vegetables are softened.

In another saucepan, melt the butter, then add the flour and blend, over low heat, for 3 or 4 minutes until smooth. Slowly add the cream, stirring constantly with a wooden spoon or whisk, for about 15 minutes until the roux is thick and smooth. Add the sauce to the tomato stock. Blend thoroughly, then add the salt and pepper.

Pour the soup into bowls and garnish with the chopped tarragon. Serve warm.

**Note:** This is a very thick, hearty soup. If you wish a thinner variation, substitute milk for half the cream. Also, this soup is equally delicious garnished with fresh chives or basil, or served cold, garnished with parsley or chives.

*Cream of tomato soup, seasoned with basil.*

85

*Chives add a subtle garlicky flavor to soups.*

© Amy Reichman/Envision

## Shaker Herb Soup

Makes 4 servings

This is a quintessential herbed soup, developed by Ronald Johnson for his fine book, *The American Table.*

*2 tablespoons butter*
*1 cup minced inner celery stalks with leaves*
*2 tablespoons minced chives*
*2 tablespoons minced fresh chervil*
*2 tablespoons minced fresh sorrel*
*½ teaspoon minced fresh tarragon*
*4 cups chicken stock*
*Salt and freshly ground pepper*
*Pinch of sugar*
*A few drops of lemon juice*
*4 slices trimmed white bread, toasted*
*Freshly grated nutmeg*
*¾ cup grated aged Cheddar*

Melt the butter in a large pot; when it stops sizzling, add the celery and chives. Cook over low heat for 5 minutes, or until the celery is soft. Add the herbs, chicken stock, salt, pepper, and sugar to taste.

Cover the pot and let simmer for 20 minutes. Taste for seasoning and add a few drops of lemon juice—the soup should be faintly tart. To serve, place a slice of toast in the bottom of each soup plate, ladle on the soup, grate a wisp of nutmeg over it, then sprinkle the cheese on top.

# Chilled Pea Soup with Mint

Makes 6 to 8 cups

*1½ cups dry green split peas, washed and*
*    picked over*
*4 cups salted water*
*4 cups chicken broth*
*1 small onion, sliced*
*1 rib celery, chopped*
*2 cloves garlic, crushed*
*1 large sprig of fresh mint*
*Salt*
*2 cups heavy cream*
*Fresh mint leaves, finely chopped*

Bring the peas to a boil in the water and boil for 5 minutes. Remove the pot from the heat and let stand, covered, for 1 hour. Drain. Add the chicken broth to the peas and bring to a boil. Add the onion, celery, garlic, mint sprig, and salt to taste. Reduce the heat, cover, and simmer until the peas are tender. Put the vegetables and broth through a food mill or process in a blender until smooth.

Chill the soup for 24 hours. When ready to serve, stir in the chilled cream. Pour into individual bowls and garnish with chopped mint.

© M. Kaufman/FPG International

**Chilled pea soup is hearty, refreshing, and delicious.**

## Low-Calorie Chicken with Tarragon

Makes 4 servings

*4 large chicken breasts, about ¼ pound each*
*Salt*
*Freshly ground pepper*
*2 tablespoons chopped fresh tarragon*
*Juice of 1 lemon*
*1 cup dry white wine*

Preheat oven to 350 degrees F (177 degrees C).

Remove all the skin from the chicken breasts and rinse under cool water, pulling off any additional fatty membranes. Place the breasts in a shallow roasting pan, and sprinkle with the salt and pepper to taste and the tarragon. Pour the lemon juice and the wine over the breasts.

Cover the pan with aluminum foil and roast for 35 minutes or until the chicken is tender and cooked through. Remove foil and bake for 5 to 10 more minutes until the chicken turns a golden brown.

Place the chicken on a warm serving dish, pour over about ½ cup of the cooking liquid, and serve.

## Chicken Breasts with Garlic, Rosemary, and White Wine

Makes 4 servings

*2 tablespoons butter*
*2 tablespoons high-quality olive oil*
*3 cloves garlic, peeled and left whole*
*4 large chicken breasts (about ¼ pound each)*
*    rinsed with cool water and dried*
*1 tablespoon chopped fresh rosemary*
*Salt*
*Freshly ground pepper*
*½ cup dry white wine*

In a skillet, heat the butter and oil. Add the garlic and chicken breasts, skin side down. When the chicken is browned on one side, turn the pieces over and add the rosemary.

When the chicken is browned on both sides, add salt and pepper to taste, and the wine. Allow the wine to boil for 2 to 3 minutes, then reduce the heat, cover the pan, and simmer for about 30 minutes. Turn the chicken occasionally to prevent it from burning. If the cooking liquid evaporates, add 1 or 2 tablespoons of water or wine.

Transfer the chicken to a warm serving platter. Pour the cooking juices over the chicken and serve.

*Opposite: Tarragon chicken can also be served with a favorite sauce.*

© Steven Mark Needham/Envision

*Coriander leaves and seeds
give this dish its unique flavor.*

## Lemon Sole with Coriander and Lime

Makes 4 servings

*1½ pounds lemon sole fillets (or any meaty white
    fish, such as flounder)*
*2 tablespoons fresh lime juice*
*Salt*
*¼ cup olive oil*
*⅔ cup heavy cream*
*2 tablespoons chopped coriander leaves*
*½ teaspoon coriander seeds*
*Sprig of fresh coriander*

Cut the fillets into 1-inch (2.5-cm) strips.
Sprinkle them with lime juice and salt to
taste.

In a skillet, heat the oil and gently sauté
the fillets, turning them frequently for 4 to
5 minutes or until cooked. Remove with a
slotted spoon.

Remove any remaining oil and wipe the
skillet clean with paper towels. Pour in the
cream and add the chopped coriander
leaves and the coriander seeds. Bring to a
boil and simmer for 2 minutes. Return the
fish to the pan and heat through. Spoon
onto a warm serving dish and garnish with
a sprig of coriander.

## John Hadamuscin's Herbed Salmon Loaf

Makes one 9 × 5 × 3-inch loaf

My friend, John Hadamuscin, is one of the most creative cooks I know. He combines his sophisticated knowledge of contemporary cooking with his nostalgic memories of his Midwestern childhood. This recipe is from his delightful book, *Special Occasions.*

*1 cup fine, dry bread crumbs*
*4 large eggs, separated*
*1 cup milk*
*6 cups flaked poached salmon or 3 15½-ounce*
*    cans red salmon, picked over and flaked*
*2 teaspoons lemon juice*
*¼ teaspoon freshly ground black pepper*
*2 tablespoons chopped fresh dill*
*2 scallions, white and green parts, finely chopped*
*2 tablespoons chopped fresh parsley*
*1 cup uncooked fresh or frozen peas*
*3 tablespoons butter, melted*

Preheat the oven to 350 degrees F (177 degrees C). Lightly grease a 9 × 5 × 3-inch (23 × 13 × 7.5-cm) loaf pan.

Combine all the ingredients except the egg whites, the peas, and 1 tablespoon of the butter in a large bowl and mix well with your hands. Mix in the peas. In a separate bowl, beat the egg whites until stiff but not dry. Fold a few tablespoonfuls of the salmon mixture into the egg whites, then fold the egg whites into the salmon mixture.

Spoon the mixture into the greased loaf pan. Place the pan in a larger shallow pan filled with 1 inch of boiling water and put both pans into the oven. Bake for about 50 minutes, or until the center of the loaf is firm and the surface is lightly browned.

Remove the pan from the oven and brush the surface of the loaf with the remaining melted butter. Let rest for 10 minutes in the pan, then remove the loaf from the pan and cool to room temperature on a wire rack. Cut into ¼-inch (.6-cm) slices just before serving.

***Note:*** The salmon loaf also can be served hot as a main course, sliced and garnished with sour cream and chopped dill or scallions.

*Fresh or frozen peas give this very special meatloaf a very special flavor.*

91

© Steven Mark Needham/Envision

*Fresh tarragon and parsley give this dish a unique color and flavor.*

## Softshell Crabs with Tarragon and Parsley

Makes 4 servings

*8 to 12 softshell crabs*
*Flour for dredging*
*8 tablespoons (1 stick) butter, plus 2 or 3*
    *tablespoons*
*3 tablespoons high-quality olive oil*
*Salt*
*Freshly ground pepper*
*2 tablespoons chopped fresh parsley*
*1 tablespoon chopped fresh tarragon*
*1 cup blanched almonds*
*Lemon wedges*

Dredge the crabs in the flour. In a large, heavy skillet, heat 1 stick of the butter and the oil until hot. Sauté the crabs over moderate heat until they are browned on one side. Turn, and brown on the other side. Add salt and pepper to taste. Sprinkle with the parsley and tarragon, then transfer to a warmed platter.

Melt the remaining butter in the skillet. Add the almonds and toast for a minute or two, and spoon over the crabs. Garnish with lemon wedges. Serve immediately.

# Classic British-Style Roast Beef

Makes 2 servings per rib

Roast beef evokes images of a quietly elegant English restaurant, like the famous Simpson's on the Strand, with the fragrance of fine roasted beef in the air combined with the sounds of tinkling crystal and silver. A fine rib roast, served rare, with horseradish sauce is an old-fashioned—yet timeless—treat.

*A 2- to 4-rib roast of beef, without the short ribs*
*Flour*
*Salt*
*Freshly ground black pepper*

Preheat oven to 350 degrees F (177 degrees C). Place the roast in a shallow roasting pan and sprinkle with a little flour. Lightly rub the flour into the fat, and season with salt and pepper to taste. Place a tent of aluminum foil loosely over the top of the meat.

Place the roast in the preheated oven and roast for about 8 to 10 minutes per pound. (Use a meat thermometer; rare beef is the most flavorful.) Serve warm with horseradish sauce.

© Burke/Triolo

# Horseradish Sauce

Makes 1 cup

*1 cup heavy cream*
*Grated fresh horseradish, to taste*
*1 teaspoon high-quality mustard*

With an electric mixer, whip the cream until it forms peaks. Gently fold in the horseradish and mustard. Place in a serving dish and serve with roast beef.

*Hearty roast beef with tangy horseradish sauce has come back into culinary style.*

## Leg of Lamb with Tarragon Cream Sauce

Makes 10 to 12 servings

The herbs most commonly associated with lamb are mint (remember Mom's mint jelly) and rosemary. However, a leg of lamb—served with new potatoes, baby asparagus, and this tarragon cream sauce—is a delicious change of pace and makes a special springtime feast. This recipe was inspired by Anne Seranne, one of my favorite cooks.

*6- to 7-pound leg of lamb*
*2 cloves garlic, sliced*
*Flour*
*1 teaspoon salt*
*Freshly ground pepper*
*1 teaspoon dried tarragon*
*2 onions, quartered*
*2 cups boiling water*
*1 tablespoon chopped fresh tarragon*
*1 cup heavy cream*

Preheat oven to 450 degrees F (232 degrees C).

Place the lamb in a shallow roasting pan, fat side up. Make deep incisions in the meaty parts of the leg and insert a sliver of garlic in each incision. Tuck any remaining garlic under the roast. Sprinkle the lamb with 2 tablespoons flour, the salt and pepper to taste, and the dried tarragon. Arrange the quartered onions around the roast.

Place the lamb in the hot oven and roast for 20 minutes. Reduce the heat to 350 degrees F (177 degrees C) and roast for 1 hour and 10 minutes. (Roasting time is 1½ hours total.) The meat will be rare; if you prefer it medium-rare, you should roast for 15 minutes longer.

Place the roast on a warm serving platter.

To make the sauce, pour off all but 4 tablespoons of the fat from the pan, leaving the charred onion. Place the roasting pan on the stove with the heat off and stir in 6 tablespoons flour. Add 2 cups boiling water and stir rapidly with whisk or wooden spoon until smooth.

Add the fresh tarragon. Turn heat on to medium. Cook the gravy, stirring in all the bits of meat glaze from the pan. When the sauce has thickened, allow it to boil rapidly for 2 or 3 minutes, then gradually stir in the heavy cream.

Correct the seasoning, and if the sauce is too thick add a bit more boiling water. Strain the gravy through a sieve into a sauce boat and serve with the lamb.

# Herbed Hamburgers

Makes 4 hamburgers

*1 pound lean ground beef*
*1 large egg, lightly beaten*
*1 teaspoon finely chopped fresh basil*
*1 teaspoon finely chopped fresh tarragon*
*1 teaspoon finely chopped fresh sweet marjoram*
*1 tablespoon finely chopped fresh parsley*
*Salt*
*Freshly ground black pepper*
*1 large onion, minced*
*3 tablespoons high-quality olive oil*
*¼ cup bread crumbs*

In a large bowl, mix together the meat, egg, herbs, and salt and pepper to taste.

In a heavy pan, sauté the onion in the olive oil until translucent. Add the onion and the oil to the meat mixture. Add the bread crumbs and combine thoroughly.

Shape into patties and sauté, broil, or barbecue. Serve on toasted buns.

© Steven Mark Needham/Envision

*Grilling hamburgers with herbs is a sophisticated way to prepare a classic dish.*

## Susan Costner's Thyme-Marinated Roast Pork

*Pork marinated in this thyme-flavored sauce is incredibly delicious.*

Makes 6 servings

Susan Costner is a marvelous cook whose recipes reflect her Southern heritage and her current California lifestyle. This recipe comes from her special book, *Good Friends, Great Dinners.*

*3 cloves garlic, peeled*
*¼ cup finely chopped fresh parsley*
*1 tablespoon dried thyme (3 tablespoons fresh thyme)*
*1 tablespoon high-quality olive oil*
*Salt*
*1 cup dry white wine*
*1 5- to 7-pound boneless pork loin*
*Freshly ground black pepper*
*1 small onion, finely chopped*
*2 cloves garlic, peeled and finely minced*
*1 cup tomato sauce, preferably homemade*
*1 tablespoon unsalted butter*

In the bowl of a food processor fitted with a steel blade or in a blender, process the 3 cloves garlic, the parsley, thyme, olive oil, 1 teaspoon of salt, and 1 tablespoon of the wine to a smooth paste.

With a sharp knife, make small slits in the meat. Force a generous quantity of the paste into the slits. Rub the remaining mixture all over the roast. Place the pork in a large roasting pan and pour on the remaining wine. Cover and marinate refrigerated for several hours, or overnight, turning the meat several times.

Preheat the oven to 400 degrees F (203 degrees C).

Drain off and reserve the wine. Sprinkle the top of the roast with salt and pepper to taste and roast for 10 to 15 minutes. Lower the oven temperature to 325 degrees F (167 degrees C) and cook for approximately 2 hours more or until a meat thermometer reads 185 degrees F (85 degrees C), approximately 35 minutes per pound. Transfer the roast to a heated serving platter, and keep the roast warm.

Pour off all but 2 tablespoons of fat from the roasting pan. Add the onion and remaining garlic and sauté gently for 2 to 3 minutes. Place the pan over high heat and deglaze the pan with the reserved wine. Add the tomato sauce and cook until the liquid is reduced by about half. Remove from the heat and swirl in the butter. Correct the seasoning with salt and pepper. Carve the roast into thin slices and serve with spoonfuls of the sauce.

## Pasta with Fresh Basil Sauce

Makes 4 servings

This pesto sauce freezes well.

*½ cup pine nuts*
*3 cups fresh basil leaves, stems removed, washed,*
*and coarsely chopped*
*2 cloves garlic, chopped*
*4 tablespoons chopped fresh parsley*
*¼ cup high-quality olive oil*
*Salt*
*4 tablespoons (½ stick) unsalted butter, softened*
*½ cup (about 4 ounces) freshly grated Parmesan*
*cheese*
*1 pound fettucini, spaghetti, or other pasta of your*
*choice*
*Grated Parmesan cheese to sprinkle on cooked*
*pasta*

To make the pesto sauce, place the pine nuts and leaves in a blender and process until coarsely blended but not pureed. Add the garlic and 3 tablespoons parsley and blend again. Add the olive oil and blend. Add salt to taste and the butter, and blend until it forms a smooth puree. Pour the puree into a bowl and stir in the grated cheese.

Cook the pasta until al dente, drain. Return the pasta to the pot and add the pesto sauce. Toss until well coated. Place in warmed serving dish. Serve immediately with freshly grated Parmesan cheese.

© Steven Mark Needham/Envision

**Spaghetti with pesto sauce is basil's greatest claim to fame.**

## Spaghettini with Olive Oil and Herbs

Makes 4 Servings

*1 pound spaghettini*
*Salt*
*3 tablespoons high-quality olive oil*
*2 tablespoons finely chopped fresh parsley*
*2 teaspoons coarsely chopped fresh oregano*
*2 teaspoons coarsely chopped fresh marjoram*
*Freshly ground pepper*

Cook the spaghettini in boiling, salted water until al dente. Drain, reserving ½ cup of the cooking liquid. Return the spaghettini to the pot and add the oil, herbs, reserved cooking liquid, and salt and pepper to taste.

Bring to a simmer, toss well, and serve immediately.

© M. Weiss/FPG International

*This simple dish is not only delicious but is very easy to prepare.*

## Cheese & Mushroom Tart in an Herbed Pastry Crust

Makes one 9-inch (23-cm) tart

### *Pastry shell*

*1 cup all-purpose flour, unsifted*
*½ teaspoon salt*
*8 tablespoons (1 stick) unsalted butter, chilled*
*1 egg yolk*
*1 tablespoon cold water*
*1 tablespoon fresh herbs (tarragon, dill, oregano, marjoram, or parsley—or mixture of herbs), minced*

Preheat oven to 450 degrees F (232 degrees C).

In a small bowl, combine the flour and salt. Make a well in the center, and slice in the cold butter. Add the egg yolk, 1 tablespoon water, and the herbs. Squeeze the herb mixture into a paste, then knead in the flour until all the ingredients are incorporated into a rough dough.

Roll the dough out in a circular shape until it is about 1 inch (2.5 cm) larger than a 9-inch (23-cm) pie plate. Gently place the dough onto the pie plate, letting it loosely cover the bottom and sides. Pat it gently into place with your fingers. Fold the overhanging edge under itself to make a double edge of dough. Flute the edge. Prick the bottom and sides with a fork.

Bake in the center of the preheated oven for 8 to 10 minutes or until pastry is set and beginning to brown. Remove from oven.

### *Cheese and Mushroom Filling*

*½ pound fresh mushrooms*
*½ pound Swiss cheese*
*2 tablespoons butter*
*2 tablespoons minced onions*
*6 egg yolks*
*Salt*
*Freshly ground black pepper*
*1½ cups heavy cream*

Wash, trim, dry, and slice the mushrooms. Shred the cheese. Set aside.

In a skillet, melt the butter and sauté the onions until they are transparent. Add the mushrooms and sauté over moderate heat for 5 minutes. Remove from the heat and spread the onion-and-mushroom mixture over the bottom of the partially baked pie crust. Sprinkle the shredded Swiss cheese over the mushrooms.

Place the egg yolks in a small bowl. Add the salt and pepper to taste, and stir. Gradually beat in the cream.

Preheat oven to 350 degrees F (177 degrees C). Place the prepared crust on a baking sheet and pour in the egg-and-cream mixture. In the center of the oven, bake the tart until the filling is barely set in the center, about 35 or 40 minutes. Remove from the oven and cool slightly. Serve warm.

## Omelette Provençal

Makes 2 servings

The following recipe is for a simple, herbed omelette. Most French omelette recipes do not include milk, but I prefer the added moisture in an omelette. Of course, you can substitute any herb of your choice for the Herbes de Provence.

*3 large eggs, at room temperature*
*3 tablespoons milk*
*2 tablespoons butter*
*Herbes de Provence (see page 116)*
*Salt and freshly ground pepper*

Break the eggs into a bowl, and whisk until they are about twice their original volume. Stir in the milk.

Melt the butter in a 10-inch (25-cm) skillet over medium-high heat until it bubbles. Add the eggs, but do not stir. When the eggs begin to firm up, sprinkle on the herbs, and salt and pepper to taste.

Light the broiler.

Hold the skillet above the heat source, tilting it from side to side until the edges begin to brown slightly. Pass the pan under the broiler for a few seconds, just long enough to cook the top.

Remove the pan from the broiler. Fold omelette in half and slide it out of the pan. Serve immediately.

© Steven Mark Needham/Envision

*Any number of fillings can be added to the simple herbed omelette.*

© Jeanetta Ho

*Aniseed adds a fresh and piquant flavor to pureed carrots.*

## Carrots with Fresh Aniseed

Makes 4 servings

*1 pound carrots, peeled and washed*
*1 teaspoon sugar*
*Salt*
*8 tablespoons (1 stick) butter*
*2 teaspoons finely chopped fresh aniseed leaves*
*A dash of Pernod or other pastis*

Thickly slice the carrots into a medium-sized saucepan. Add the sugar, salt to taste, and cold water to cover. Bring to a boil, cover, and cook for 15 minutes or until carrots are tender.

Drain, and puree the carrots in a blender or pass through a food mill. Return to the saucepan, add the butter, aniseed, and Pernod. Cook gently, stirring constantly, over low heat until the butter has melted and any extra water has evaporated. Spoon the carrot puree into a hot serving dish.

## Sautéed Zucchini with Garlic and Herbs

Makes 6 servings

*8 to 10 small zucchini*
*¼ cup high-quality olive oil*
*2 cloves garlic, minced*
*Salt*
*1 tablespoon chopped fresh basil*
*1 tablespoon chopped fresh oregano*
*Freshly ground pepper*
*2 tablespoons chopped fresh parsley*

Cut the zucchini into thin strips. In a heavy skillet, heat the olive oil then add the zucchini strips. Sauté lightly, turning them frequently, for about 5 minutes. Add the garlic, salt to taste, the basil, and oregano. Cook for about 10 minutes or until the zucchini are tender. Add the pepper to taste. Spoon onto a warmed serving dish and sprinkle with parsley.

## Green Beans in Cream with Parsley and Dill

Makes 6 servings

*2 pounds fresh green beans*
*Salt*
*4 tablespoons (½ stick) butter*
*Freshly ground pepper*
*1 tablespoon chopped fresh dill*
*1 cup heavy cream*
*2 tablespoons chopped fresh parsley*

Wash the beans carefully and remove any traces of string. If they are tender, leave whole; otherwise cut on a diagonal. Wash again and drain.

Bring a pan of salted water—enough to cover the beans—to a boil and add the beans. Boil for a few minutes, then reduce heat to medium and cook for 12 to 15 minutes. The beans should be crisp but not raw. Drain, and return to the saucepan with the butter. Add salt and pepper to taste. Add the dill and cream, and toss with the beans. Spoon into a heated serving dish and sprinkle with the parsley.

*© FPG International*

**Garlic and parsley add sophistication to the world's most humble vegetable.**

## Mashed Potatoes with Garlic and Parsley

Makes 6 servings

Mashed potatoes are considered to be one of the universal comfort foods. With garlic and parsley, they have a grown-up flavor without losing their childlike appeal.

*2 pounds Idaho potatoes*
*4 large cloves garlic*
*Salt*
*2 tablespoons butter*
*1 cup milk*
*2 to 3 tablespoons finely chopped fresh parsley*
*Freshly ground black pepper*

Peel the potatoes, wash under cold water, and cut into large chunks. Place in a pot with water to cover and add the garlic and 1 teaspoon salt. Bring to a boil, reduce the heat, and boil gently until the potatoes are tender, about 25 to 30 minutes.

Drain the water. Push the potatoes through a food mill or begin beating with an electric mixer. Add the butter and mix thoroughly, then add the milk, mixing until incorporated. Season with salt and pepper to taste.

## Snow Peas with Chives

Makes 6 servings

*6 tablespoons butter*
*6 pounds snow peas, trimmed*
*Salt*
*2 tablespoons finely chopped fresh chives*
*3 scallions, diced*

Melt 4 tablespoons of butter in a skillet and stir in the snow peas. Add salt to taste, cover, and cook over moderate heat for 5 or 6 minutes.

Stir in the chives and scallions, and cook gently 2 or 3 minutes more, until the scallions have softened.

Add the remaining butter, and when it has melted, serve immediately.

© Guy Powers/Envision

**Snowpeas combine well with many herbs.**

## Simple Garden Salad with Parsley Vinaigrette

Makes 4 servings

This is a basic green salad dressed with a basic French vinaigrette; however, it can be altered in endless ways. Substitute radicchio, watercress, Boston lettuce, or any number of greens for the lettuces. Add or substitute basil, rosemary, thyme, tarragon—or any herb that suits your palate—for the parsley. Finally, consider any combination of flavored vinegars (raspberry, for example) or oils (hazelnut oil might be delicious). If you have a sweet tooth, honey adds a nice consistency to the vinaigrette. The only limitation is your own creativity!

*4 to 6 cups fresh garden lettuce (bibb, leaf,*
*    romaine, butterhead, etc.), carefully washed and*
*    torn into pieces*
*1 cup arugula, washed and torn into pieces*
*1 Belgian endive, sliced*
*1 clove garlic, peeled and minced*
*2 tablespoons minced fresh parsley*
*²/₃ cup high-quality olive oil*
*3 tablespoons white wine vinegar*
*1 teaspoon grainy mustard*
*Salt*
*Freshly ground black pepper*

Dry the greens carefully and toss together in a bowl. Chill.

Whisk together the garlic, parsley, and olive oil. Whisk in vinegar; add the mustard and continue whisking until the dressing is smooth. Add salt and pepper to taste.

Pour the dressing over the greens just before serving.

*Lettuce greens and herbs are a*
*quintessential combination.*

106

## John Hadamuscin's Red Salad with Basil Mint Dressing

Makes 6 servings

As part of a Fourth of July celebration, John Hadamuscin, a native of America's heartland, often serves this salad on a blue-and-white spongeware platter to get the full colors of Old Glory.

*2 large red peppers*
*1 medium red onion, peeled and vertically sliced*
*6 large, ripe tomatoes*
*¼ cup high-quality olive oil*
*1 tablespoon red wine vinegar*
*1 tablespoon lemon juice*
*1 teaspoon capers*
*1 tablespoon chopped fresh basil*
*1 tablespoon chopped fresh mint*

Preheat the broiler. Cut the red peppers in half vertically and seed them. In a shallow pan, place the pepper halves, cut side down, along with the onion strips. Broil the vegetables until the peppers' skins start to pucker—about 5 minutes—then remove from heat.

Peel and seed the tomatoes and peel the peppers, then cut each into ¼-inch strips. Place them, along with the onions, in a large bowl.

Combine the oil, vinegar, and lemon juice in a small bowl and whisk to blend. Stir in the capers, basil, and mint and pour this dressing over the vegetables. Gently toss the salad, cover, and refrigerate for at least 2 hours before serving. Serve chilled or at room temperature.

*Tomatoes combined with basil and mint give this salad a special vitality.*

## Celery Root with Herbed Mayonnaise

Makes 6 servings

*1 cup good mayonnaise*
*2 tablespoons tarragon vinegar (see page 119)*
*3 tablespoons chopped fresh parsley*
*1 tablespoon chopped fresh tarragon*
*1 tablespoon wild celery seeds*
*3 whole scallions, finely chopped*
*1 tablespoon Dijon mustard*
*Juice of ½ lemon*
*Salt*
*Freshly ground pepper*
*1 pound (about 3 knobs) celery root*

Add all the seasonings to the mayonnaise. Set aside. Peel the celery root and slice into fine julienne. Add the celery to the mayonnaise mixture as you slice or they will turn brown. Combine thoroughly, refrigerate for several hours or overnight. Serve chilled.

## Herb Bread

Makes 3 loaves

*2 packages dry or compressed yeast*
*2½ cups warm water*
*2 teaspoons powdered chicken bouillon*
*½ cup hot water*
*3 tablespoons sugar*
*8 tablespoons (1 stick) butter, melted*
*8 to 9 cups all-purpose flour*
*1 tablespoon crushed fresh basil*
*1 tablespoon crushed fresh oregano*
*1 tablespoon crushed fresh thyme*
*½ teaspoon salt*

Combine the yeast and the warm water in a large bowl. Stir with a fork until dissolved.

In a small bowl, blend the powdered chicken bouillon and the hot water.

Blend the sugar, dissolved chicken stock, and butter into the yeast mixture. Beat in 3 cups of flour until smooth. Stir in the basil, oregano, thyme, and salt. Gradually add additional flour to make a soft dough.

Turn the dough out onto a floured surface and knead until smooth, or for about 10 minutes. Place the dough in a warm, greased bowl. Cover loosely with a towel or plastic wrap. Allow the dough to rise for about 1 hour until it is double in size.

Punch the dough down. Turn out onto a floured surface and knead for 2 or 3 min-

© Steven Mark Needham/Envision

*Herb bread can also be made in the round—it makes a very special gift.*

utes. Cover with a towel and let rest for 10 minutes.

Shape into 3 loaves and place in greased 8½ × 4½ × 2½-inch (21 × 11 × 6-cm) loaf pans. Cover and let rise until the dough reaches the tops of the pans, or about 40 minutes. Preheat oven to 350 degrees F (191 degrees C). Bake in the preheated oven for 40 minutes. Remove the loaves and set on racks to cool.

**Note:** Depending upon your taste, substitute marjoram, savory, or rosemary for the herbs suggested.

109

© James Randklev/FPG International

*Strawberries grow abundantly well and are delicious plain or with cream.*

## Wild Strawberries and Cream

Makes 4 servings

Strawberries are the universal favorite fruit. Wild strawberries are smaller and have a slightly less-sweet flavor than the large strawberries cultivated for mass production, but they are delectable. Try to serve strawberries within hours of picking.

*4 cups freshly picked wild strawberries*
*Sprigs of spearmint*
*2 cups heavy cream*

Pick over the berries, wash gently and thoroughly in cool water, and divide evenly among 4 serving dishes. Keep refrigerated until serving time. Garnish each dish with a sprig of spearmint. Pass a pitcher of heavy cream.

**Note:** Wild strawberries can also be served with crème fraiche or with a dash of Grand Marnier.

## Summer Fruit Compote

Makes about 6 cups

This subtle fruit compote with the interesting addition of tarragon was created by Chef Waldy Malouf of the Hudson River Club in New York City.

*1 cup sugar*
*¼ cup honey*
*1 vanilla bean*
*½ cup water*
*1 cup raspberries*
*1 cup strawberries (sliced in half)*
*1 cup blueberries*
*2 apricots, peeled, pitted, and cut into 4 pieces each*
*1 stalk rhubarb*
*½ cantaloupe cut into balls*
*2 tablespoons chopped fresh mint*
*1 tablespoon chopped fresh tarragon*

In a saucepan, mix together the sugar, honey, vanilla, and water and bring to a boil. Reduce heat and simmer for 5 minutes. Remove the vanilla bean, and add all the fruit and simmer for another 5 minutes. Cool. Add the fresh herbs. Chill well.

Serve as is in small bowls with cookies or over ice cream or cake, such as Rozanne Gold's Wine Cake (see page 112).

© Brian Leatart

***Dessert compotes can be made using a variety of fruits.***

# Rozanne Gold's Wine Cake

Makes 1 tube cake

Rozanne Gold is a well-known New York restaurant consultant. Her delicious wine cake makes a perfect accompaniment to the Summer Fruit Compote (see page 111).

*4 cups sifted all-purpose flour*
*2 cups sugar*
*1 tablespoon baking powder*
*1 teaspoon salt*
*Grated rind of 1 lemon*
*4 large eggs, lightly beaten*
*1 cup dry white or red wine*
*⅔ cup vegetable oil*
*½ cup crushed sugar cubes*
*2 tablespoons crushed fresh mint*
*1 tablespoon chopped fresh rosemary*

*Fresh herbs, especially peppermint, give this cake a unique flavor.*

Preheat oven to 350 degrees F (177 degrees C). Grease and flour a 10-inch (25-cm) tube pan.

In a bowl, combine the flour, sugar, baking powder, salt, and grated lemon rind. Make a well, and add the eggs. Stir lightly with a wooden spoon until mixture is crumbly.

In a small bowl, combine the wine and oil. Add the liquid to the flour mixture in 4 batches, beating lightly to incorporate the liquid thoroughly. Pour the batter into the tube pan. Sprinkle the crushed sugar cubes and herbs on top and bake for 1 hour. Check with a cake tester for doneness. Cool on a rack.

## Patty Layne's Oranges with Lemon Leaves and Cointreau

Makes 4 servings

*15 to 20 lemon verbena leaves*
*1 cup Cointreau*
*4 large, firm navel oranges, chilled*

Reserve 8 of the best-looking lemon verbena leaves. Mash the remaining leaves and add to the Cointreau and allow them to infuse the liquor for about 1 hour.

Peel the oranges and divide them into sections, removing as much of the white pulp as possible. Place into 4 serving bowls. Pour the Cointreau over the oranges. Garnish each bowl with 1 or 2 lemon leaves.

Serve immediately with Melissa's Shortbread Cookies (see page 114).

© L & M Photo/FPG International

*Oranges combine surprisingly well with many herbs— especially lemon verbena.*

## Melissa's Shortbread Cookies

Makes about 2 dozen cookies

*8 tablespoons (1 stick) unsalted butter*
*1/4 cup sugar*
*1 1/2 cups all-purpose flour*
*2 teaspoons finely chopped fresh lemon balm leaves*
*1 teaspoon fresh sweet cicely leaves*
*A little extra sugar*

Preheat oven to 325 degrees F (167 degrees C).

Cream the butter with the sugar until smooth. Work in the flour and the herbs to make a soft dough then shape into a ball. Roll out the dough on a floured surface until 1/4-inch (.6-cm) thick and cut out rounds using a 2-inch (5-cm) cookie cutter.

Bake on a greased baking sheet for 15 to 20 minutes or until the cookies begin to change color. Cool the cookies on a wire rack, then sprinkle with sugar.

## May Wine Punch

Makes about 24 cups

*1/2 cup sweet woodruff leaves*
*2 tablespoons wild strawberry leaves*
*2 tablespoons meadowsweet leaves*
*Juice of 2 lemons*
*3 bottles of Johannesburg Reisling, May wine or other Rhine wine*
*1/2 cup sugar*
*1 bottle sparkling white wine or Champagne*
*10 to 12 wild strawberries*

Dry the sweet woodruff, wild strawberry, and meadowsweet leaves in a dark cupboard for a few hours. Remove stems and place leaves in a punch bowl. Add lemon juice and about 1/2 bottle of the white wine, and allow the leaves to marinate in the juice for 3 to 4 hours. Add the sugar and another 1/2 bottle of white wine. Chill. Just before serving, add the remaining white wine and the sparkling wine and float a few strawberries on the top.

# Herb Blends

## Bouquet Garni

The classic bouquet garni is used often in French cooking to flavor stews, soups, and sauces. Depending upon the dish, the bouquet garni can be varied to include appropriate herbs, but the one that follows is classic and is suitable for most dishes. The herbs can be fresh or dried.

Makes 1 bouquet

*2 sprigs parsley*
*1 bay leaf*
*¼ teaspoon thyme*

Cut a small, about 3-inch (7.5-cm) square of cheesecloth. Place the herbs in the center of the square, gather the edges, and wrap a length of strip or twine around the bundle to knot it.

**Note:** During the Christmas holidays after you have dried herbs, consider making a number of bouquets garnis, using a variety of herbs. Label each bouquet with its contents—or its suitable dish—place several in a glass jar, box, or plastic bag, and give as a much-appreciated gift to your favorite gourmand.

© Amy Reichman/Envision

**A bouquet garni** *made of sage, tarragon, and rosemary tied together with twine.*

*Opposite: Lovely pots containing personalized herbal combinations can be bought throughout Provence in France.*

## Fines Herbes

Makes about 1 cup

This strongly flavored combination of herbs and spices is excellent for flavoring meat loaves, pâté—and even a humble hamburger. Consider adding a pinch to a strong-flavored vegetable such as broccoli or to a cheese omelette or quiche.

*1 tablespoon whole cloves*
*1 tablespoon freshly grated nutmeg*
*1 tablespoon broken pieces of cinnamon stick*
*1 tablespoon chopped fresh thyme*
*1 tablespoon chopped fresh basil*
*1 tablespoon chopped fresh oregano*
*1 tablespoon chopped fresh savory*
*3 bay leaves, broken in pieces*
*2 teaspoons whole black peppercorns*

Place all the ingredients in a spice grinder or blender and pulverize them into a fine powder. Store in an airtight jar or freeze in a plastic bag.

## Herbes de Provence

Makes about ½ cup

There are many recipes for herbes de Provence because the herbs characteristic to Provence are numerous and the possibilities for delicious combinations are endless. The following is a simple recipe, very good for use on grilled fish, in soups and stews, or on vegetables.

*2 tablespoons dried thyme leaves*
*1 tablespoon dried rosemary leaves*
*1 tablespoon dried savory leaves*
*½ teaspoon dried lavender leaves*

Powder all the ingredients together in a blender, food processor, or by hand with a mortar and pestle. Store in an airtight container or in a plastic bag.

**Note:** Herbs most commonly associated with Provence include basil, bay, savory, coriander, lavender, marjoram, oregano, rosemary, savory, and thyme. Combine them in any way you wish to create your own personal version of herbes de Provence.

# Herbed Butters

This is a good, basic herbed butter, delicious on fish, poultry, or vegetables.

*8 tablespoons (1 stick) unsalted butter*
*1 tablespoon lemon juice*
*Salt*
*Freshly ground pepper*
*1 tablespoon chopped fresh parsley*

Cream the butter, then beat in the remaining ingredients. Place the butter on a piece of plastic wrap and shape into a tube; or spoon into a crock and cover with plastic wrap. Chill.

This butter will stay fresh in the refrigerator for 2 weeks or will freeze for up to 3 months.

### Variations:

Variations to herbed butters are virtually infinite and depend upon the dishes you are cooking or your particular tastes. Here are a few suggestions:

**Garlic butter:** Add 2 minced cloves garlic to the basic recipe. Garlic butter is especially good on potatoes, toasted bread, and pasta.

**Chive butter:** Using the basic recipe, substitute chives for the parsley. This is

particularly tasty with egg dishes and vegetables.

**Tarragon butter:** Substitute tender young tarragon leaves, finely minced, for the parsley in the basic recipe. Tarragon is always delicious on chicken and fish.

**Beurre de Provence:** Substitute 1 finely minced shallot and 1 tablespoon of herbs de Provence for the parsley in the basic recipe. Beurre de Provence is delicious on grilled fish and chicken and is perfect with vegetables.

*Herbed butters are easy to make and enhance many dishes.*

118

# Herb Vinegars

Many herbs, either alone or in combination, make fine vinegars. Herbs can also be combined in vinegar with strong-flavored vegetables such as garlic, hot pepper, or shallots for a pungent taste. Store herb vinegars in decorative 16- or 32-ounce (450- or 900-ml) bottles that are readily available at kitchenware shops. Rebottle the vinegars to make them more attractive, especially if they are to be given as gifts. After the vinegar has aged, strain it through cheesecloth, add a fresh, attractive herb cutting to the bottle, and rebottle the strained liquid.

© Steven Mark Needham/Envision

*Herbed vinegars stored in decorative bottles.*

### Red Wine Vinegar

Makes 1 pint

*1 pint (16 ounces) red wine vinegar*
*2 or 3 sprigs of oregano*
*1 or 2 garlic cloves, crushed*

Pour the vinegar into a small saucepan. (Avoid using an aluminum pan.) Heat the vinegar over medium heat to just below simmering and remove the pan from the heat.

Place the herbs and the garlic into a sterilized 16-ounce bottle. Ladle the warm vinegar into the bottle and seal with a cork or tight-fitting lid. Place the jar in a cool, dark place to age for 3 to 4 weeks before using.

This recipe can be easily doubled.

### Tarragon Vinegar with Lemon Balm

Makes 1 pint

*1 pint (16 ounces) white wine vinegar*
*2 or 3 fresh tarragon leaves*
*2 lemon balm leaves*
*1 or 2 cloves garlic, crushed*

Follow the directions for preparing Red Wine Vinegar, above.

## Herb Oils

Herb-flavored oils are delicious for use in cooking or in salad dressings. Combinations of herbs that make flavorful oils are infinite and are made even more complex by the various flavors of the oils. For example, subtly flavored herbs such as chervil combine better with less-robust oils such as safflower oil, whereas stronger herbs such as garlic or tarragon are tastier in a heartier oil such as olive oil or sunflower oil. Also, when making oils, consider adding other ingredients such as lemon, lime, capers, peppercorns, or ginger to the oil for more complex flavors.

### Basic Method

In a bottle with a tight-fitting cork or lid, place 2 or 3 sprigs of your favorite herb and any other ingredient of your choice such as capers or peppercorns, then funnel in 2 cups of high-quality vegetable oil. Leave the bottled oil in a warm place, like a sunny window sill, for at least 3 days. (The longer the oil steeps, the more strongly flavored it will be.) Strain the infused oil, rebottle, and store in a cool place.

## Herbal Teas

### Soothing Chamomile Tea with Lemon Verbena

Makes 6 cups

This is a flavorful "sleepytime" tea, to settle jangled nerves or even an upset stomach.

*3 to 4 teaspoons crushed chamomile leaves*
*3 to 5 teaspoons crushed lemon verbena leaves*
*6 cups boiling water*
*Sugar and cream to taste*

Place the herbs in a teapot or tea caddy and pour the hot water over the leaves. Allow the tea to steep for about 2 minutes. Pour while the tea is still very hot, and add cream and sugar if desired.

*Herb teas also can be combined in an infinite number of ways to make soothing or invigorating brews.*

# Highland Thyme-Flavored Tea

Makes 6 cups

Ancient Scottish warriors believed that thyme-flavored tea would provide them with the strength and courage to face battle. This pungent tea, sweetened with sweet woodruff, a hint of heather, and honey, will provide a morning pick-me-up and allow today's warriors to face the battle of everyday life.

*2 tablespoons thyme leaves, crushed (lemon thyme*
*can be substituted)*
*1 teaspoon crushed sweet woodruff*
*¼ teaspoon crushed heather flowers*
*6 cups boiling water*
*Cream to taste*
*Honey to taste*

In a warmed teapot, add the crushed thyme leaves, sweet woodruff, and heather, and pour in the boiling water. Allow the tea to steep for 2 to 3 minutes, then pour. Add cream and honey to taste.

# GLOSSARY OF GARDENING TERMS

**acid:** A term applied to soil with a pH content of less than 6.5.

**alkaline:** A term applied to soil with a pH content of more than 7.3. Most herbs prefer alkaline soil.

**annual:** A plant that grows from seed, flowers, and then dies in one growing season.

**biennial:** A plant that takes two growing seasons to complete its life cycle.

**bud:** A young, undeveloped flower, although it can also denote a leaf or shoot.

**compost:** A blend of decomposed organic matter, which is sometimes combined with soil or sand and used to nourish plants.

**creeping:** A term used to describe a plant that trails over the ground or over other plants.

**cross-pollination:** The transfer of pollen from one plant to another.

**cultivar:** A cultivated variety of plant (as opposed to one that occurs naturally in the wild).

**cutting:** A leaf, bud, or part of a stem or root that is without roots. It is removed from a plant and potted to form the basis of a new plant.

**deadhead:** Withered flowers that should be removed to prevent seeding.

**deciduous:** A plant that drops its leaves at the end of the growing season; the opposite of an evergreen.

**disbud:** To remove buds from flowers to encourage foliage growth.

**division:** To propagate by dividing roots or tubers into sections that are then replanted and form separate plants.

**drainage:** The act or method of draining water from a garden plot or container.

**drying:** A method of preserving herbs, seeds, and flowers by placing them in the open air for a period of days or weeks. Herbs may also be dried in a microwave oven.

**evergreen:** A plant that bears living foliage all year-round.

**genus** (plural: genera): The classification of a group of closely related plants belonging to the same family.

**half-hardy:** A term applied to annual plants indicating that plants so described will grow outdoors but may not survive frost.

**hardy:** A term applied to certain plants indicating that they will tolerate freezing conditions (annuals) or will survive a cold winter without protection (perennials).

**herbaceous:** A term usually applied to perennial plants whose stems are not woody and which die down at the end of each season.

**humus:** Partly or wholly decomposed vegetable matter that is used to nourish garden soil.

**hybrid:** A plant that results from a cross between two parent plants belonging to different species, subspecies, or genera.

**infusion:** A concoction derived from pouring boiling liquid (water, oil, vinegar) over herbs and letting it steep for a given length of time.

**invasive:** A term used to

describe plants that spread (often including their roots) quickly and easily from their original site.

**loam:** Humus-rich soil containing up to 25 percent clay and less than 50 percent sand.

**mulch:** A covering—either organic or man-made—laid down to protect plant roots, hold moisture, control temperature, and control weeds.

**peat moss:** Partially decomposed moss, rich in nutrients and with high water retention capabilities, which is often added to garden soil to add nourishment.

**perlite:** A substance (literally a natural volcanic glass) used to enhance soilless mediums for starting seeds and cutting, or added to garden soil to enhance drainage.

**perennial:** A plant that

lives from year to year. The stems and leaves of a perennial die down in winter, but new shoots appear each spring.

**pH scale:** A system, measured on a scale of 1 to 14, devised to measure the acid/alkaline content of soil. Soils that register below 7 are acid; those above 7 are alkaline.

**pinch:** To remove leaves from a plant to encourage branching and growth.

**pistil:** The seed-bearing or female organ of a flower.

**propagate:** The process of reproducing plants.

**prostrate:** A term used to describe plants that lie on the ground, creep, or trail.

**rootstock:** The crown and root system of herbaceous perennials and shrubs. The term is also used to describe a vigorous plant onto which another plant is grafted.

**runner:** A stem that spreads along the soil surface, rooting wherever it comes into contact with moist soil and creating new plants.

**self-seed:** A term applied to plants that drop their seeds around them from which new plants grow; self-sow.

**shrub:** A perennial whose stems and branches are woody and grows only a few feet high.

**sow:** To propagate new plants from seed.

**species:** A classification applied to plants within a genus.

**stamen:** The male, pollen-bearing part of a flower.

**subshrub:** A small shrub whose base (trunk) stem is woody but whose stems are soft.

**thin:** To weed out thickly planted growing areas, and

allow plants to grow with sufficient surrounding space. Plants can be removed and thrown away, or replanted elsewhere.

**till:** To work the soil into small fragments where seeds or seedlings can be planted.

**topiary:** Evergreen trees and shrubs that have been clipped into geometric or other ornamental shapes.

**tuber:** A root or underground stem in which food is stored.

**variety:** A term applied to a naturally occuring variation of a species of plant.

**vermiculite:** A mineral substance used together with peat moss and perlite to create a sterile soilless medium for starting seeds and cuttings.

**weed:** An unwanted plant in a lawn or garden. A rose bush may be considered a weed in a vegetable patch.

## HERBAL SOCIETIES

These professional gardening societies can provide useful information. If you write to any of the following organizations, include a self-addressed, stamped envelope to ensure a reply.

American Herb Associates
Box 353
Rescue, California 95672

Herb Research Foundation
Box 2602
Longmong, Colorado 80501

The Herb Society of America
2 Independence Court
Concord, Massachusetts 01742

## MAIL-ORDER SOURCES

The following centers or companies supply seeds, plants, and gardening accessories. Write for a catalogue. Check your local Yellow Pages under "Herbs" for suppliers in your area.

Berkshire Garden Center
Routes 102 and 183
Stockbridge, Massachusetts 01262

W. Atlee Burpee & Co.
Warminster, Pennsylvania 18974

Brooklyn Botanic Garden
1000 Washington Avenue
Brooklyn, New York 11225

Casa de Luz Herbs
3568 S. Campbell Avenue
Tucson, Arizona 85719

Cruickshank's Inc.
1015 Mt. Pleasant Road
Toronto, Ontario, Canada
M4P 2M1

Dominion Seed House, Ltd.
115 Guelph Street
Georgetown, Ontario, Canada
L7G 4A2

Gardener's Eden
P.O. Box 7307
San Francisco, California 94120

Gardenimport
P.O. Box 760
Thornhill, Ontario, Canada
L3T 4A5

Hancock Shaker Village
Gardenimport
P.O. Box 760
Thornhill, Ontario, Canada
L3T 4A5

P.O. Box 898
Pittsfield, Massachusetts 01202

Otto Richter & Sons, Ltd.
Box 26
Goodwood, Ontario, Canada
L0C 1A0

Tansy Farm
5888 Else Road
Agassiz, British Columbia, Canada
V0M 1A0

White Flower Farm
Litchfield, Connecticut 06759

# SUGGESTED READING

## Gardening Books

*Better Homes and Gardens* Editors, *Better Homes and Gardens' Complete Guide to Gardening.* Des Moines: Meredith Corporation, 1979.

Bremness, Lesley, *The Complete Book of Herbs.* New York: Viking Studio Books, 1988.

Bookes, John, *The Garden Book.* New York: Crown Publishers, Inc., 1984.

Bookes, John, *The Indoor Garden Book.* New York: Crown Publishers, Inc., 1985.

Brookes, John, *The Small Garden.* New York: Crown Publishers, Inc., 1989.

Crockett, James Underwood, *Crockett's Victory Garden.* Boston: Little Brown & Company, 1977.

Dietz, Marjorie, *The ABC's of Gardening.* Garden City: Doubleday and Company, 1985.

Halpin, Anne M., *The Window Box Book.* New York: Simon & Schuster, 1989.

McNair, James K., *The World of Herbs & Spices.* San Francisco: Ortho Books, 1978.

Page, Mary and Stern, William T., *Culinary Herbs.* London: The Royal Horticultural Society, 1974.

Reader's Digest Editors, *Reader's Digest Illustrated Guide to Gardening.* Pleasantville: *Reader's Digest* Association, 1981.

Reilly, Ann, Consulting Editor, *Taylor's Pocket Guide to Herbs and Edible Flowers.* Boston: Houghton Mifflin Company, A Chanticleer Press Edition, 1990.

Stevenson, Violet, *Growing Herbs Successfully.* London: Tiger Books, 1980.

## Cookbooks

Costner, Susan, *Gifts of Food.* New York: Crown Publishers, Inc., 1984.

Costner, Susan, *Good Friends, Great Dinners.* New York: Crown Publishers, Inc., 1987.

Gubser, Mary, *Mary's Bread Basket and Soup Kettle.* New York: William Morrow & Company, 1974.

Hadamuscin, John, *Special Occasions.* New York: Harmony Books, 1988.

Holt, Geraldene, *Recipes from a French Herb Garden.* New York: Simon & Schuster, 1989.

Johnson, Ronald, *The American Table.* New York: William Morrow & Company, 1984.

Lang, Jennifer Harvey, *Tastings.* New York: Crown Publishers, Inc., 1986.

Waters, Alice, *Chez Panisse Pasta, Pizza & Calzone.* New York: Random House, 1984.

# INDEX

Grateful acknowledgment is given to the following sources for use of their recipes in this book:

"Herb Bread" from *Mary's Bread Basket and Soup Kettle* by Mary Gubser. © 1975 by Mary Gubser. By permission of William Morrow & Company, Inc.

"Shaker Herb Soup" from *The American Table* by Ronald Johnson. © 1984 by Ronald Johnson. By permission of William Morrow & Company, Inc.

"Thyme-Marinated Roast Pork" from *Good Friends, Great Dinners* by Susan Costner. © 1987 by Susan Costner. By permission of Crown Publishers, Inc.

"Red Salad with Basil-Mint Dressing" and "Herbed Salmon Loaf" from *Special Occasions* by John Hadamuscin. © 1988 by John Hadamuscin. By permission of Harmony Books, a division of Crown Publishers, Inc.

"Summer Fruit Compote" © 1990 by Chef Waldy Malouf, The Hudson River Club, New York City.